IDOLS

Amish is a 1974-born, IIM (Kolkata)-educated banker-turned-author. The success of his debut book, *The Immortals of Meluha* (Book 1 of the Shiva Trilogy), encouraged him to give up his career in financial services to focus on writing. Besides being an author, he is also an Indian-government diplomat, a host for TV documentaries, and a film producer.

Amish is passionate about history, mythology and philosophy, finding beauty and meaning in all world religions. His books have sold more than 7 million copies and have been translated into over 20 languages. His Shiva Trilogy is the fastest-selling and his Ram Chandra Series the second-fastest-selling book series in Indian publishing history. You can connect with Amish here:

- www.facebook.com/authoramish
- www.instagram.com/authoramish
- www.twitter.com/authoramish

Bhavna Roy was educated in Mussoorie, Pune and Mumbai. After graduating in psychology from Mumbai University, she qualified for the Indian Administrative Services. Having trained partly at the LBSNAA, she quit and then worked first as a volunteer in a school for special children in Malegaon, and then in an NGO in Nashik called SOS. She is the wife of the late Himanshu Roy IPS. She lives in Mumbai.

Celebra
30 Years of F
in India

T0182556

Other Titles by Amish

SHIVA TRILOGY

The fastest-selling book series in the history of Indian publishing

The Immortals of Meluha (Book 1 of the Trilogy)

The Secret of the Nagas (Book 2 of the Trilogy)

The Oath of the Vayuputras (Book 3 of the Trilogy)

RAM CHANDRA SERIES

The second-fastest-selling book series in the history of Indian publishing

Ram – Scion of Ikshvaku (Book 1 of the Series)

Sita – Warrior of Mithila (Book 2 of the Series)

Raavan – Enemy of Aryavarta (Book 3 of the Series)

War of Lanka (Book 4 of the Series)

INDIC CHRONICLES

Legend of Suheldev

NON-FICTION

Immortal India: Young Country, Timeless Civilisation

Dharma: Decoding the Epics for a Meaningful Life

'{Amish's} writings have generated immense curiosity about India's rich past and culture.'

– Narendra Modi
(Honourable Prime Minister of India)

'{Amish's} writing introduces the youth to ancient value systems while pricking and satisfying their curiosity …'

– Sri Sri Ravi Shankar
(Spiritual Leader and Founder, Art of Living Foundation)

'{Amish's writing is} riveting, absorbing and informative.'

– Amitabh Bachchan
(Actor and Living Legend)

'Amish is one of India's greatest storytellers, creative, imaginative, so you have to turn the page.'

– Lord Jeffrey Archer
(One of the highest-selling authors of all time)

'{Amish's writing is} a fine blend of history and myth … gripping and unputdownable.'

– BBC

'Thoughtful and deep, Amish, more than any author, represents the New India.'

– Vir Sanghvi
(Senior Journalist and Columnist)

'{Amish} is an extraordinary gift to the world from India. He has done a great service by taking ancient myths and giving them relevance in modern times.'

– Deepak Chopra
(World-renowned Spiritual Guru and Bestselling Author)

'{Amish is} one of the most original thinkers of his generation.'
— *Arnab Goswami*
(*Senior Journalist and MD, Republic TV*)

'Amish has a fine eye for detail and a compelling narrative style.'
— *Dr Shashi Tharoor*
(*Member of Parliament and Author*)

'{Amish has} a deeply thoughtful mind with an unusual, original and fascinating view of the past.'
— *Shekhar Gupta*
(*Senior Journalist and Columnist*)

'To understand the New India, you need to read Amish.'
— *Swapan Dasgupta*
(*Member of Parliament and Senior Journalist*)

'Through all of Amish's books flows a current of liberal, progressive ideology: about gender, about caste, about discrimination of any kind… He is the only Indian bestselling writer with true philosophical depth – his books are all backed by tremendous research and deep thought.'
— *Sandipan Deb*
(*Senior Journalist and Editorial Director, Swarajya*)

'Amish's influence goes beyond his books, his books go beyond literature, his literature is steeped in philosophy, which is anchored in bhakti, which powers his love for India.'
— *Gautam Chikermane*
(*Senior Journalist and Author*)

'Amish is a literary phenomenon.'
— *(Late) Anil Dharker*
(*Senior Journalist and Author*)

AMISH
& BHAVNA ROY

IDOLS
UNEARTHING THE POWER
OF MURTI PUJA

HarperCollins *Publishers* India

First published in India by HarperCollins *Publishers* 2023
4th Floor, Tower A, Building No. 10, DLF Cyber City,
DLF Phase II, Gurugram, Haryana – 122002
www.harpercollins.co.in

2 4 6 8 10 9 7 5 3 1

P-ISBN: 978-93-5699-450-8
E-ISBN: 978-93-5699-451-5

Typeset in 11/16.2 Sabon LT Std at
Manipal Technologies Limited, Manipal

Printed and bound at
Thomson Press (India) Ltd

To my wife, Shivani

Grief and suffering over time numb you,
Till you simply stop feeling,
And plaster a smile on your face to hide your pain.

Then someone teaches you to be happy again,
And smile, even when you are alone.

Shivani, my saviour, my shelter from the storm, my
reason to smile.

—Amish

To my sisters-in-law Meeta, Donetta and Shivani,

My friends, my confidantes,
My sweetest ringfence, my strongest support

My sisters beyond the bounds of Law,
For you are more than in-laws.

You bring joy to my brothers,
A steadiness to their lives,
And solidity to my world—my family.

My three Goddesses.

I will cherish you till the day I die.

—Bhavna

CONTENTS

ACKNOWLEDGEMENTS

The late Vinay Kumar Tripathi: father to Amish and Bhavna; you taught us what to be and what not to be. The late Himanshu Roy: husband to Bhavna, brother-in-law to Amish; a guide to both, a man beyond compare. The late Dr Manoj Vyas: father-in-law to Amish, uncle to Bhavna; a fount of wisdom for both. Their honour, grace and dignity continue to inspire us. You dwell in our hearts.

Neel, Amish's young son. You have always been my greatest love. But, with every passing year, as I see your strong and compassionate character emerge, you have also become my greatest pride.

Shivani, Amish's wife. My strength in my personal life. My ally in my working life. The magic string who holds it all together.

Anish, Meeta, Ashish and Donetta, our siblings and sisters-in-law, for always being there. Our rocks of Gibraltar.

The rest of our family: Usha, Sharda, Surendra, Pankhuri and Siddharth. For their constant faith and love.

The children of the family: Mitansh, Nikita, Daniel, Varun, Aiden, Keya, Yash, Anika and Ashna, our joy and our future.

Neel's mother, Preeti, and her family Shernaz, Smita, Anuj, Ruta, for their consistent support.

Aman, who drives Amish's business activities, and is like a brother to both of us.

The team at HarperCollins. My editor Poulomi; Shabnam and the entire marketing team led by Akriti; Gokul, Vikas and the entire sales team led by Rahul; the copy editor Shreya; the digital marketing team led by Ameya; the Harper360 team—Karen, Serena, Darren, and Sinead; all led by the brilliant CEO of HarperCollins India, Ananth, guided by Charlie Redmayne, the CEO of HarperCollins UK, Ireland, India and Australia. The partnership with them goes from strength to strength, as they take our books all over the world.

The team at Pratilipi. Gautam, the CEO; Karthika, the editor; and the rest of the team, which brings out the Indian regional language editions of this book. Karthika was also the first editor of the first draft of *Idols*, when she was in Westland.

Navin, Anu, Nitin, Vishal, Avni, Mayuri, Khushi, Annie, Pia. For being Bhavna's family of the heart.

Sivan and Yaron Barzilay, Bhavna's gurus. I will always be grateful to you. You taught me life and living.

Sneha Datar, an accomplished poetess in Marathi, Urdu and English, for her poems and her constant love and support.

Anu Alahari, for helping us flesh out the three principles each of the *Pravruttic* and *Nivruttic* impulses. They came to life in a series of uplifting conversations.

Nimmu Kishnani, for giving us access to the thesis by Thakkar Harish Gopalji, under the guidance of Dr Manjiri Bhalerao—'Lord Jhulelal: An analytical study'.

Vijay, Shubhangi, Padma, Divya, Shaurya and the rest of Amish's colleagues at his offices in Mumbai and London. They take care of the business, which gives him enough free time to write.

Mehul, who looks after Bhavna's personal office. He enables her to live a purposeful life.

Hemal, Neha, Rohan, Hitesh, Shikha, Parth, Mridu, Aakash, Vinit, Harsh and Team OktoBuzz. They have made most of the marketing material for the book and all the digital activities.

Ashish Mankad, a super-talented designer and, more importantly, a thinker, who helps guide and drive the art for Amish's books.

Sandeep, Caleb, Dominic, Akhil and their respective teams, who support Amish's work with their business, legal and marketing advice.

Mrunalini, a Sanskrit scholar, who works with us on research.

Aditya, a passionate reader of Amish's books, who has now become a friend to both Bhavna and Amish, and also a fact-checker.

Sanjay, Archana, Sandeep, Pranjulaa, Olivier, Ravichandran, Vineet and Somnath, who are a part of Amish's team at Nehru Centre, London, and Harish, Nidhi, Valli, who are a part of Amish's Education team at the Indian High Commission in the UK, for their love and support.

And last, but certainly not the least, you, the reader. Your consistent affection, understanding and encouragement are what we deeply cherish. Thank you so much. May Lord Shiva bless all of you.

FOREWORD

The idea for this book emerged from three incidents.

The first incident happened with me (Amish). I was on the stage at a popular literature festival, and the audience largely comprised youngsters—the primary audience of my books. One college-going youth stood up and said that he liked my books and that he was a proud Hindu, but not an 'idol-worshipper obviously'. He said that last bit almost with distaste. I stopped him before he could get to his question and asked what was 'obvious' about not being an idol-worshipper. He said that he knew that idols were not real Gods and worshipping them was wrong, and, hence, did not do it. And then he reiterated, 'But I am a proud Hindu.' I was 'obviously' befuddled by the youth's contradictory comments and wanted to question him further. But I thought it best not to challenge him in a public forum and in front of his friends and let him get on with his question. However, the incident remained in my mind. This book is, in a way, a response to that youth, who is interested in our culture, but has, perhaps, not completely understood it. He is suffering from a version of what psychologists call 'battered-wife syndrome', in which the wife, suffering violence at the hands of her husband, often blames herself as the cause of the violence. Idol-worshippers, as a group, have suffered horrific violence over the past 2,000 years and the worst genocide in human history; they have been wiped out almost everywhere in the world, except for a few remaining outposts like India. Yet, like battered wives, there are many idol-worshippers today who blame themselves, rather than those who oppressed their ancestors.

The second incident happened when both of us (Bhavna and Amish) saw something on a social media platform. An Indian journalist (publisher of a fashion magazine) publicly wrote that the 'destruction of idolatry' is a 'good fight to fight'. And he seemed to draw a direct correlation between immoral/unjust societies and idolatry. The key thing wasn't the historical inaccuracy of this claim; for both idol-worshipping and idol-rejecting cultures have enough examples of sometimes creating unjust/immoral societies. The key thing was that the said journalist proclaimed himself as a humanist, who was seeking a just, kind and green world. This book is, in a way, a suggestion to that journalist to explore how idol-worshipping often leads to a just, kind and green world. Because there are many idol-rejecting cultures (primarily European Christians and Turkic Muslims) who went around the world massacring tens of millions of people, destroying thousands of temples along with tens of universities, and wiping out entire civilizations, for the supposed crime of idol-worshipping.[1] But there are almost no examples of the reverse, i.e., almost no idol-worshipping culture has gone around the world wiping out civilizations for their refusal to worship idols. And a green world? Remember, among idol-worshippers, nature is not a resource to be exploited, but a Goddess to be worshipped. That's why idol-worshippers make for natural environmentalists and supporters of a green world.

The third incident happened during a get-together at our home. We had a friend over, who got really agitated when we used the term 'idol-worshipping'. She said, quite aggressively, that *murti puja* is not idol-worshipping. And then she went into describing minute details about how the two terms are different. She also pointed out that because we use the term 'idol-worshipping', Westerners portray us as 'backward and violent pagans'—similar to the ancient Central Americans, European Celts and Vikings—which, according to our friend, we Hindus are not. We tried to explain that if we accept the framing of the debate as done by the idol-rejecting cultures over the last two millennia, and say that they should blame ancient Central Americans, Celts, Vikings and other pagans for the 'crime' of idol-worshipping, rather than us Hindus since we are different, it would be insulting to our ancestors and the global community of idol-worshippers of the past. We need to point out, calmly but forthrightly, that the framing of the debate, as idol-worshipping being 'wrong', is itself erroneous. We are not sure that we were able to convince the friend that evening. This book is another, more detailed attempt to do so.

But let's make a few things clear. This book is not trying to say that idol-worshipping is superior to other forms of spirituality/religiosity. It is not a for-or-against kind of book. If you don't want to believe/participate in *murti puja* (*idol-worshipping*), don't do it. There are certainly areas of improvement in the idol-worshipping ways, just as there are comforts and strengths. The same is true for idol-rejecting cultures. But we want to explain why both of us are proud idol-worshippers; and, why *murti puja* gives us peace.

Furthermore, we certainly would like to differentiate between people and ideas. Our experience has been that most people are, on average, decent. Having pre-existing biases against people—be they an individual or group—is wrong, and must be called out for what it is, i.e., bigotry. But this should not preclude an honest appraisal of ideas or ideologies; for ideas drive the behaviour of crowds— both in positive and negative directions.

This book is structured as conversations, drawing inspiration from the ancient Indian Upanishadic traditions and the Greek Socratic Dialogues authored by his student, Plato. We find that conversations are a much better way to explain complex concepts than the relatively modern Western approach of a non-fiction book, which ends up being rather textbook-ish. The conversations in this book should be seen as a network of ideas and not a linear progression. We feel that idol-worshipping can provide solace and support in life. Through *bhakti* (*devotion*), it can lead to the experience of surrender, joy and fraternity. It can also serve as an invaluable tool for self-understanding and self-realization. This is possible through the Hindu concept of *Ishta Devata* (*Chosen Gods*). We have tried to flesh out the symbolic essence of the philosophy of *Ishta Devata*, and explored the idea that we can, thus, unearth ourselves and then, through transformation, arrive at abundance, steadiness and love. Idol-worshipping can also, over time, enable us to ultimately experience, and not just intellectually or ideologically know of, the Oneness of God. To Dharmics (Hindus, Buddhists, Jains and Sikhs) this is the unitary Godhood of Brahman and encountering the truth that the Gods and Goddesses are a subset—a part—of Oneness. Brahman.

This book is a sequel to our previous non-fiction book, *Dharma*, with an expanded cast of characters conversing and debating with each other. You can read *Dharma* first, or this one. The sequence does not matter. Find the path that works best for you. Also, please note that when we have quoted ancient texts or stories, we have paraphrased them, to make them understandable for the modern reader.

शैववैष्णवशाक्ताश्च बौद्धजैनादयस्तथा ।
धर्मस्य सन्ति पन्थानः लोके लोके च नैकशः ॥
तेष्वेकतमं कमपि वृत्वा मोक्षस्य कारणम् ।
चरैवेति चरैवेति दृढं शास्त्रस्य शासनम् ॥

Shaiva, Vaishnava, Shaakta, Bauddha, Jaina, and many others,
Multiple paths of Dharma do avail in this wide world.
Tradition says: Choose one or more than one,
The chosen path is not important, for the end of all the paths is Moksha.
What is important, is to walk your chosen path.

चरैवेति चरैवेति ।
Keep Walking.
Keep Walking.

—**Bhavna and Amish**
London and Mumbai, 2023

Shaiva = Path of Lord Shiva; Vaishnava = Path of Lord Vishnu; Shaakta = Path of the Mother Goddess (Shakti); Baudha = Path of Gautam Buddha; Jaina = Path of the Tirthankars.

1

MATTERS OF
THE HEART

Dharma Raj Deshpande woke up with an uneasy feeling. Massaging his chest, he reached for his bedside clock. 2.30 a.m. He tried to prop himself up but collapsed on the pillow. He touched his wife lightly. Lopamudra was instantly awake. 'What's the matter?' she asked, concerned.

'We must go to the hospital,' Dharma Raj mumbled. Lopamudra sprang off the bed and reached for her phone.

Nachiket Anant Sawant stretched out his arm to reach for his phone. He shook his wife, Gargi's, shoulder when he read the name flashing on the screen. *Sasurji (father-in-law)*. Ten minutes later, the young couple were on the road. Nachiket dialled his friend Anirban.

Thirty minutes later, the family was on its way to Peaches and Pearl Hospital, with Nachiket behind the wheel. Tense silence prevailed. Three months earlier, Dharma Raj had suffered a mild heart attack and the doctor had warned him against overexerting himself.

Dharma Raj was a retired police officer of the elite Indian Police Service, Maharashtra cadre. He was the quintessential cop—tough and physically intimidating, but also diligent and kind in his dealings with people. The remarkable thing, as his wife, Lopamudra, often said, was that his job had not hardened his eyes. They were always full of compassion and love. She was immensely proud to be his wife. He was her 'man-mountain'. Lopamudra, in turn, was his rock, strength and oasis. She restored his faith in human nature, he said. His job exposed him excessively to the ugliness and negativity of life. His personal life with Lopamudra was a constant reminder of its immeasurable beauty. They sat together now, in the back of the car. Lopamudra held her husband's large hand in her small hand. Yet, they somehow fit. Rhythmically, he pressed the base of her thumb with his own. It hurt, but she did not move her hand away.

Nachiket sat with a stony expression, intent on his task—to reach the hospital as soon as possible. Gargi sat beside him, staring out of the window. Over the years, Nachiket had come to look up to his father-in-law as his guru, his sanctuary, as well as his guiding light in the path of life. Someday the qualities of his master would meld into his own being, he knew. That was his destiny. For now, he strived to stay the course.

Suddenly, a biker careened in front of the car. Nachiket slammed the brakes, and the biker came to a screeching halt in front of the car. 'Sorry, Papa,' he muttered under his breath. He was furious as he threw open the door and rushed at the biker. The biker removed his helmet and seemed unhurt, and stared at Nachiket insolently. Nachiket moved rapidly to slap the biker hard across the face, twice. The biker fell off the bike, with an incredulous expression on his face, then quickly jumped back on and took off in a hurry. Nachiket flicked his right hand a couple of times to calm himself down and walked briskly back to the car. As he got in, he stole a glance at his wife. Her expression was withdrawn. Also, accusing. Nachiket started the car. Lopamudra looked at her son-in-law's back with compassion brimming in her eyes, even as she suppressed her anxiety at having lost a few seconds in the rush to the hospital. She looked at her husband. She saw sadness and understanding, but no judgement. Dharma Raj closed his eyes.

They drove directly into the portico of Peaches and Pearl Hospital, where Anirban was waiting for them. A valet took their car away. As they entered the lobby, they spotted the idol of Lord Ganesh prominently mounted on a platform to their left. Nachiket quickly kneeled and placed his forehead on the ground with reverence before the idol. Gargi smiled as she looked at the man she loved. As usual, she had tuned out his earlier loss of control. She placed her right hand on her chest. Anirban narrowed his eyes and observed his friend, bemused.

They rushed into the Emergency Room. Anirban had called Dr Adarsh Bhattacharya, Pune's eminent

cardiologist and his childhood friend, as soon he had
received that call from Nachiket. The doctor was also
Dharma Raj's cardiologist.

Dr Adarsh had informed the Emergency department
and the nursing staff on duty in advance to receive the
patient. They made Dharma Raj lie down on a slim bed
and checked his vitals: blood pressure and temperature.

The family and Anirban moved into the reception area.

After the ECG (electrocardiogram) was done, Dharma
Raj was wheeled away on a stretcher to the Radiology
department for a CT (computerized tomography) scan.

After an hour, Dr Adarsh called Nachiket on his
phone. The CT scan was clear. The doctor on duty
had also sent the ECG report to him, and there was
nothing to worry about. In all likelihood, it was a case
of acute acidity. Dr Adarsh recommended Dharma Raj
be admitted in the hospital for observation and had
already asked the nursing staff to administer an IV dose
of Pantoprazol. He wanted Dharma Raj to be examined
by a gastroenterologist in the morning. He also wanted
to repeat the ECG after six hours, along with the Trop
T (Troponin T) test. The doctor wanted to proceed with
abundant caution.

Nachiket relayed the message to his family.

Lopamudra: '*Devaa chi krupa!* (*Thank God!*)'

There was palpable relief all around.

Dharma Raj was wheeled out on a stretcher with drips attached. The IV needle had been inserted into a vein on the back of his left hand. The IV solution was set at the rate of thirty drops per minute, Lopamudra noted. It would take a couple of hours for the dose to be completed.

'It seems I'll live. More's the pity!' He winked at his wife. Lopamudra discreetly scrunched her face and stuck her tongue out at him. Dharma Raj smiled.

He was wheeled to the ninth floor, where a room was made ready. Lopamudra accompanied him.

The rest of the party completed the paperwork and payment details, and took the elevator to the ninth floor, to room number 909. It was a suite, actually.

Nachiket laughed as the three young people entered the room. 'Papa, honestly, you needn't have frightened us in the middle of the night to get me to introduce Anirban to you.'

Everyone laughed.

Nachiket: 'This is Anirban Kothapalli, a freelance photographer. Anirban, my Papa—my freelance guru!'

Anirban laughed. 'Freelance guru! Unattached to any guru-led organization! I'll hire you, Uncle!'

Gargi: 'And this is my mother, Anirban—Lopamudra Mondal Deshpande.'

Anirban looked at the old lady, startled by the information.

Anirban: 'Are you Bengali, Mrs Mondal? I mean, Mrs Deshpande?'

Lopamudra: '*Hyan, aami Bangali.*'

Gargi: 'She said *"Yes, I'm Bengali"*, in Bangla.'

Anirban smiled at Gargi and then looked at Lopamudra. '*Aami bhablaam aapni Maharashtriyan. (I assumed you're Maharashtrian.)*'

Lopamudra: 'I've been Maharashtrian too, for all my adult life. But how do you know Bangla?'

Anirban: 'Just a smattering. I have known Adarsh since early childhood and spent a lot of time in his home. I was exposed to more Bangla than Telugu, almost!'

Lopamudra: 'Interesting.'

Dharma Raj: 'What are you doing in Pune? You live in Mumbai, don't you?'

Anirban: 'I'm here on an assignment. A small photoshoot, on Ganeshotsav.'

Lopamudra: 'Yes, of course. The day after is Shukla Paksha Bhadrapada Chaturthi.'

Anirban: 'Saturday, you mean; so, the day after the day after tomorrow. I thought I'd catch up with Nachiket and Gargi, so I came a couple of days early. Also, Adarsh.'

Lopamudra: 'It's 3.30 in the morning, Anirban. "Tomorrow" has begun. Today is Thursday, not Wednesday anymore.'

Anirban: 'Of course ... What did you just say? Shukla Paksha ...?'

Lopamudra: 'It's a bit complicated, but if you are going to be shooting the event, you might as well know the basics of the utsav.'

We know that the Moon revolves around the Earth, while the Earth revolves around the Sun. The Western Gregorian solar calendar is based exclusively on the movement of the Earth around the Sun. The Arab Islamic lunar (Hijri) calendar, on the other hand, is based exclusively on the movements of the Moon. Of course, all calendars also factor in the rotation of the Earth and Moon on their own axes. These calendars have, thus, kept their calculations simple, but missed out on some portions of the whole truth of Time. The Hindu calendar is lunisolar[2]. It accommodates the movements of both the Sun and the Moon. It covers more truth of Time, but not all, for it is not for us humans to claim the whole truth; including that of Time.

More truth makes the Hindu calendar more complex.

Each lunar month (usually a period of one new moon to the next, which is approximately 29.5 days) is divided into two fortnights (which is around 14.77 days). Shukla Paksha is the bright fortnight of the waxing moon, from one day after the night of Amavasya (no moon) to Purnima (full moon) night. Krishna Paksha is the fortnight of the waning moon. It is the dark fortnight, beginning from one day after Purnima to Amavasya—the night of no moon.

Hindus observe two types of lunar months:

1. In the Amavasyanta (Amavasya-Anta or No Moon-End) system, the month ends on a no moon day. This system is used in South, West (Gujarat and Maharashtra) and East (West Bengal, Assam and Tripura) India. The first day of the new moon to full moon (Shukla Paksha) and then to no moon (Krishna Paksha) is one Amavasyanta month.

2. In the Purnimanta (Purnima-Anta or Full Moon-End) system, the month ends on a full moon day. This system is used in north India and Odisha. The first day after the full moon to the no moon (the dark fortnight) and then to the full moon (the bright fortnight) is one Purnimanta month.

There are twelve lunar months of 29.5 days, adding up to a total of 354 days in a lunar year. To adjust the calendar to the solar year of 365 days, the gap of about 11 days per year is adjusted once every three years, through the *adhik maas* (*extra month*). The *adhik maas* is inserted to align the lunar and solar calendars, hence the Hindu calendar is lunisolar. The *adhik maas* would be added in 2023 Shravan, 2026 Jyeshtha, 2029 Chaitra,

2031 Bhadrapada, 2034 Ashadh, and so on. This month is also called *Purushottam maas* since Lord Vishnu presides over this month instead of the twelve zodiac signs. Since no celebratory events like weddings take place in the *adhik maas*, it is also called *mal maas*, devoted to charity and prayers.

The *adhik maas* is added when a lunar month both begins and ends before Surya Deva moves to the next zodiac in the constellation.

A *tithi*, loosely speaking, is equivalent to one full day in a lunar month. A *tithi* is a twelve-degree movement of the Moon, relative to the earth-sun axis. And Chaturthi is the fourth day, or *tithi*, in both the light and dark fortnight. Charturdashi is the fourteenth day in both Shukla Paksha and Krishna Paksha.

Bhadrapada is the sixth month of the Hindu calendar. The fourth day of the bright fortnight of Bhadrapada—Shukla Paksha Bhadrapada Chaturthi—is Ganesh Chaturthi. Ten days later is Anant Chaturdashi, or Shukla Paksha Bhadrapada Chaturdashi. Between this Chaturthi and Chaturdashi is the ten-day Ganeshotsav, the festival of Lord Ganesh.

Anirban: 'Wow! I didn't know this at all. Aunty, you must explain this to me in more detail one day.'

Lopamudra: 'I will be glad to do so.'

Nachiket looked at his wife. 'Adarsh will visit at 9 a.m. I suggest we visit around that time. We will meet the gastroenterologist as well, I presume.'

Gargi: 'Sounds good. We should leave now and head back home. You can come dressed for work and go straight to Ego, Nachiket.'

Ego, the oddly named hotel where Nachiket worked as a sous chef, was located just a bit away from the hospital, on the same road.

Anirban: 'I will come as well. I haven't met Adarsh as yet. And I'll come to meet you again, Aunty and Uncle.'

Nachiket: 'Hmmm … Ma, Papa, we'll see you in the morning.'

Saying so, the three young people left the room.

2

AN AUSPICIOUS BEGINNING

Anirban, Nachiket and Gargi walked into Suite 909 at 8.45 a.m. the next day. They found the old couple seated in companionable silence. Lopamudra was reading. Dharma Raj looked contemplative. Lopamudra greeted them, then got up and moved to the antechamber. 'I'll get some tea ... made with teabags, I'm afraid,' she said. Nachiket went along with his mother-in-law to help.

Lopamudra: 'You can chat, people. We can hear you.'

Nachiket: 'And will join you when needed.'

Dharma Raj: '*Kasa kaay, mandali? (How are you doing, young people?)* What's your day going to be like?'

Gargi: 'I've already had a hectic start since 5.30 in the morning; we have hardly slept. I drove Nachiket away from the study into the living room and interrupted his morning "me-time". Anirban, the study doubles up as my workplace. I've finished two advanced classes before coming here. I have two more classes lined up for the day. Tiring ... I intend to do some reading in the afternoon.'

Nachiket smiled to himself as he dipped a teabag in a cup.

Gargi Sawant was a Yoga instructor. Ebullient and irrepressible, she was Nachiket's delight, his mood-uplifter. She did not view the world from a cynical lens or by looking too deep into human beings, and took them at face value. Innocent, untouched by life and its games, she was his 'wonder woman'. Nachiket gave in to periodic phases of dark, lonesome and brooding behaviour, but only the people closest to him saw him this way ever. To everyone else, he was a bright, cheerful and empathetic person. Cooking had always quietened his mind and pleased the sensual aesthete in him. Gargi called him deep and dishy, almost unreadable at times.

Five minutes later, Nachiket and Lopamudra appeared with cups of hot tea for everyone.

Nachiket: 'I began the day with Bappa (Lord Ganesh)—at 3.30 in the morning, here in the hospital. I'll end it with a modak line-up at work.'

Lopamudra: 'Do you need to get to work soon? Are you getting late?'

Nachiket: 'That's all right. It's an easy start to the day. I think we'd all like to spend some time with the two of you.'

Dharma Raj: 'Music to my ears. And you, Anirban? What will your day look like?'

Anirban: 'I will spend some time preparing for the shoot. Visit the site. If I can manage it, I might read a little in the late afternoon.'

Dharma Raj: 'What are you reading?'

Anirban: 'P.G. Wodehouse. A Bertie Wooster story.'

Dharma Raj smiled. He said, 'My favourite as well. I only read Wodehouse and Wilbur Smith.'

Gargi: 'That's what he wants everyone to think. And then he quotes Woody Allen or Rumi. Sometimes Oscar Wilde, too!'

Lopamudra: 'Or Groucho Marx and Pu. La. Deshpande!'

Everyone laughed.

Anirban: 'Let's leave Pelham and Wilbur alone. I'd love to hear your thoughts on matters less serious for now.'

Dharma Raj laughed. He turned to his daughter and said, 'Hmmm ... What are you reading these days, Gargi?'

Gargi: 'I'm reading Catherine Nixey's *The Darkening Age*, Papa. It's quite amazing. Alarmingly amazing, I mean. But look at this, I just saw it in today's *Sakal*.[3] An unfortunate incident around Ganeshotsav. I don't know if you've read about it. It made me feel bad.'

Ganeshotsav is a ten-day period of religious festivity in India, especially in the state of Maharashtra.

The fourth day of the waxing moon in the month of Bhadrapada is Ganesh Chaturthi. It is the day Lord Ganesh visits us mortals. He dwells in our homes, our minds and our hearts. On Anant Chaturdashi, *Bappa*, our *father*, leaves us heartbroken on the fourteenth day of the waxing moon.

When or how did the festival begin in India? No one knows. There are records of Ganeshotsav celebrations in Pune during the reign of the mighty Maratha, Chhatrapati Shivaji Maharaj, in the seventeenth century. The Peshwas continued the tradition of public celebration in the eighteenth century. The British brought an end to both official and elite patronage around the beginning of the nineteenth century, and drove all Hindu public religious celebrations indoors. The arrival of Lord Ganesh, thus, became a private family affair. But it sustained. It survived.

Towards the end of the nineteenth century, public celebrations roared back into the collective consciousness of the Indians. Bal Gangadhar Tilak, our beloved Lokmanya, revived the festivities. It was his response to the passing of a legislation banning mass gatherings of Hindus in public. His newspaper *Kesari* hailed the Sarvajanik Ganeshotsav, and Lokmanya dedicated his efforts towards organizing grand events in the month of Bhadrapada—from Shukla Paksha Chaturthi to Anant Chaturdashi.

On Ganesh Chaturthi, Lord Ganesh and His mother, Goddess Gauri, leave their abode atop Kailash Parbat

(Mount Kailash) and enter the homes and hearts of their devotees as *atithi devas* (*godly guests*). Clay idols of the mother and child are ceremonially placed and decorated in homes. *Sarvajanik Mandals*[4]—social groups that come together to publicly celebrate the Ganesh festival—place idols of Lord Ganesh in public places. Events are organized in elaborate pandals or tents during the ten days. Daily prayers and rituals are conducted and prasad is distributed to one and all.

The ten days fly by in a flash and it's time for Bappa to leave us and go back to His family—His father, Lord Shiva, and His brother, Lord Kartikeya. His mother, Goddess Gauri, is there as well, for She had left for home earlier on the sixth or seventh day of the celebration, as Her family needed Her back home on Kailash Parbat. With sweet grief and boisterous chanting, the Lord is immersed in a body of water—the sea, a stream, a pond, and so on.

The *visarjan* (*immersion*) on Anant Chaturdashi is a massive event in cities like Mumbai. Lakhs of devotees throng the beaches and bid goodbye to their beloved God—in full knowledge that He will be back the following year.

They all scream in unison, '*Pudchya varshi laukar ya!* (*Hurry back next year!*)'

Dharma Raj: 'What is the story about?'

Gargi: 'A group of boys belonging to a Sarvajanik Mandal—I forget which one—spent the day collecting funds from the locality. Late in the evening, the cops found them creating a ruckus on the street. Drunk and disorderly, you would have officially called it, right, Papa?'

Anirban: 'Honestly, I often wonder—is all this hoopla really about faith? Does God even inhabit the Lord Ganesh idol? Any idol, really?'

Nachiket: 'Try not to debunk a practice that goes back centuries over a single random incident in a single random locality.'

Anirban: 'True, true. I hear you. I'm not trying to draw any quick conclusions. A few young boys behaving badly one evening is not reflective of society. I get that—'

Dharma Raj: 'But the way you phrased your comment—you were referring to faith.'

At that moment, Dr Adarsh Bhattacharya entered the room. 'Hello Uncle. Aunty … Anirban! It's been a long time!' He shook his friend's hand, and then hugged him warmly. He turned to Nachiket and Gargi. 'Forgive me. I'm meeting him after … four years?' He turned and looked at Anirban.

Anirban nodded.

Gargi: 'He has come to Pune after a very long time. We usually meet in Mumbai.'

Dr Adarsh walked up to the patient.

Dr Adarsh: 'Uncle, I've spoken with Dr Phadnis. She's the gastroenterologist. She will see you at 11 a.m., but I think she has already asked for stool examination to look for occult blood. She would like to rule out ulcers in the stomach. If the acidity does not settle by the afternoon ...'

Dharma Raj: 'I must admit, Adarsh, I'm still uncomfortable. It is not settling down.'

Dr Adarsh: 'Hmmm ... she might do a gastroscopy. She has also asked for another dose of Pantoprazole to be given intravenously. Let's see. I think you're going to be in the hospital today. You should be able to go home tomorrow morning. We will do another ECG as well. And the Trop T test. Now that I have you here, I'm going to pull out all the stops!'

Dharma Raj: 'I'm safe in your hands.'

Gargi: 'Looks like we're going to be in this room this evening. Adarsh, join us if you can. Even if it's for a bit.'

Dr Adarsh: 'Let's see. Uncle, the nurse will be here soon for the ECG and Trop T ... I'll head off now. Bye, everyone.'

Dr Adarsh briskly walked out of the room.

Nachiket: 'I should be leaving as well. I must get to work.'

Anirban: 'Uncle, we will continue this conversation in the evening—about deities and faith.'

Dharma Raj smiled.

Anirban: 'Gargi, can you drop me to my hotel?'

Gargi: 'Yep, let's go.'

Anirban, Gargi and Nachiket left soon thereafter.

3

DECLINE OF WISDOM; RISE OF FAITH

Nachiket and Anirban stepped off the elevator on the ninth floor of Peaches and Pearl Hospital at 7 p.m. Nachiket greeted the nurses standing at the nursing station. 'Hello, Sister Madhuri. How are you, Sister Anungla?'

The nurses smiled warmly at him. The men turned and entered Suite 909.

Gargi had already arrived and was sitting on a slim sofa placed against a wall, reading a book. Lopamudra sat on a sofa chair placed next to her husband, who sat propped up on the bed. Lopamudra held a magazine in her hands. Dharma Raj held his phone, answering messages.

Nachiket: 'Namaskar *karto*, Papa. Ma, namaskar. Hi Gargi.'

Anirban: 'Good evening, Uncle and Aunty. Hello Gargi.'

Gargi: 'Hello, hello, hello. What took you so long, Nachiket?'

Nachiket: 'Too much work ... But it's only seven in the evening.'

'Tea, everyone?' Lopamudra walked into the antechamber without waiting for a reply. Gargi followed her mother.

Dharma Raj: 'You don't look very tired, Nachiket. Nor do you, Anirban.'

Anirban: 'We don't look half as fresh as you, Uncle. You look well rested.'

Dharma Raj: 'I can't wait to get back home. I'm tired of this place.'

'We will head back in the morning,' Lopamudra called out. 'Your acidity has settled down. They've already put you on oral antacids.'

Dharma Raj: 'Not a moment too soon! I meant for getting back home, not the antacids. It's Ganesh Chaturthi day after tomorrow. We will leave early in the morning, Lopa.'

'I've taken care of the payments, Papa. You can leave early tomorrow morning,' Gargi said as she walked into the room with cups of tea on a tray. She handed a cup to her father. Anirban and Nachiket picked their cups.

There was a moment of peace and silence as everyone settled down with their tea. Lopamudra sat in the chair near her husband, lightly holding his hand. Anirban settled on a chair near the TV cabinet, and Gargi and Nachiket sat down at opposite ends of the room.

Lopamudra: 'Anirban, you look as if you want to say something. *Bol do! (Say it!)*'

Anirban: 'Is it so obvious? Actually, our conversation was left hanging at an intriguing point, Uncle.'

Dharma Raj: 'And what was that? Remind me. I remember Gargi mentioning an article in *Sakal*. And that she is reading an alarming book!'

Dharma Raj's eyes rested on his daughter with fond indulgence. Nachiket shook his head imperceptibly. Gargi preened and then stuck out her tongue at her husband. He raised his eyebrows, then smiled.

Anirban: 'I had talked about the idea of God—Gods inhabiting idols, and you said I had referred to the idea of faith ...'

Lopamudra laughed, and said: 'Now you're in for it, Anirban.'

Gargi: 'Dangling conversations! Yay!'

Nachiket's eyes twinkled as he recited the lines from Simon and Garfunkel's song 'Dangling Conversations'. '"... As the sun shines through the curtain lace. And shadows wash the room!" Yes! Papa, this setting is too perfect.'

Gargi: 'Anirban, Nachiket is proposing an extended conversation here in this hospital.'

Nachiket: 'Why not? Endless cups of *do ghoont chai* (*two sips of tea*) and some *charcha* (*discussion*)!'

Gargi: 'Shouldn't he be resting? I'm just asking.'

Lopamudra: 'A conversation would be deeply restful for Papa, you know that. And it was just acidity, remember?'

Dharma Raj cast his wife a faintly petulant look.

Lopamudra smiled, 'Severe, yes, but acidity nonetheless.'

Nachiket: 'Great then!'

Anirban: 'This sounds interesting. Nachiket has often told me about your discussions on the subject of faith and spirituality. And it's true that I've been thinking about it of late, what with this shoot I've got myself into.'

Dharma Raj: 'So … you mentioned faith. There is nothing wrong with faith, Anirban. It provides solace, security, sanctuary, cultural grounding—that itself is meaningful.'

Anirban: 'Sometimes, I think it's just a crutch.'

Dharma Raj: 'Some people need crutches. You don't have to use them if you don't need them.'

Lopamudra: 'Faith is also related to *bhakti*. Loving devotion. It is beautiful. It expands and deepens your heart.'

Anirban: 'Okay.'

Gargi: 'You asked if God inhabits an idol. Papa, I remember you mentioned "idolatry" the last time we were talking. What do you say, shall we tackle the subject head-on?'

Lopamudra: 'It doesn't require aggression, Gargi.'

Gargi: 'Doesn't it, Ma? Look at what Anirban said. Idol worship has been systematically rubbished for 2,000 years. As if it's silly or primitive—certainly not intelligent.

Do you remember that Aamir Khan movie, Nachiket—
PK?'

Nachiket: 'Yes. I remember that scene when the
alien picks up a rock, applies paan masala on it and
scoffs that it's now ready to be worshipped. It made me
uncomfortable.'

Anirban: 'The movie is clearly making rational
arguments against idol worship. Living spiritual masters
are painted with a broad brush as false gurus. I'm not
really big on rituals and worshipping—they don't make
sense to me. But yes, the underlying implication in the
movie is that idol-worshippers are idiots. Honestly, that
scene made me squirm. It was as though my grandmother
and my mother were being insulted somehow.'

Nachiket: 'I remember reading an article about it a
long time back, written by Amish, when the movie was
released.'

Gargi: 'I know the one you are talking about. I think
it was in the *Hindustan Times*.' She picked up her phone
and googled till she found it. 'Here it is.'

Gargi: '"*Clearly,* PK *is a noble attempt to convince us
that naked, humanoid aliens regularly visit India and they
can educate us on our relationship with God. In this same
spirit of scientific inquiry,* PK *casts some serious doubts
on religion. Actually, not all religions; some have been
covered perfunctorily. The primary scholarly analysis is
on religions that practise idol worship.*"[5]

Nachiket laughed: 'Cutting sarcasm! Anyway, this belief that idol worship is primitive has been around for too long; to say that it's pre-modern, even wrong.'

Gargi: '"... *few are able to give a cogent, theological answer as to why it's wrong, except one that you can't argue with: 'My God said so!'* Hence, they had to dislike it ... And Amish continues ... *"Over the last two millennia, some communities ... took this dislike to an extreme level to end the 'Satanic' idol-worshipping practice forcibly. There was massive violence across the world to purge idol worship."'*

Lopamudra: 'This violence was a global phenomenon, actually. Europeans, Turks and many others went to great lengths to forcibly end idol worship. In their view, it was genuinely "satanic", as bizarre as that sounds to us. There was a massive effort to purge idol worship throughout the world. Temples were destroyed or appropriated, tens of millions slaughtered. So many idol-worshipping cultures—the Hellenic, the Khemic, the Mesopotamian—were almost completely annihilated. They only exist in museums now.'

Nachiket: 'Gargi, you called Catherine Nixey's book alarming. It's about this, isn't it? The Christian destruction of the pagan philosophical world?'

Gargi took the book lying beside her and held it up. 'Yes. It lasted centuries, this wanton destruction. It was horrific. You should read the way Nixey describes the destruction of the temple of Athena in Palmyra. Athena's statue at the Acropolis was also brought down. I was crying as I was reading it, Nachiket.'

Goddess Athena is the daughter of Zeus, king of the Gods, who lives on Mount Olympus. She emerged from his split forehead—as a grown woman, wearing Her armour and ready for battle[6].

One day, the Gods on Mount Olympus spot an idyllic coastal village. Who should be its patron? The contenders are too many, so Zeus decides to stage a contest between the two strongest warriors: Athena and Poseidon (Zeus's brother and God of the Seas). Who would bestow a greater gift upon the paradisal village?

Poseidon descends from Mount Olympus with Athena. They stand atop Acropolis in godly splendour. The citizens gather around the hill, silent and agog. Poseidon pulls rank and goes first. He raises his trident high and brings it down with a terrible noise. An enchanted spring of water gushes out in frolic from the spot where the trident has struck. The crowd cheers with undisguised glee. However, when some brave men step up and drink the liquid, they spit it out. The God of the Seas has gifted them salty water.

It is Athena's turn now. She raises her eyes towards the heights of Olympus, quietly goes down on her knees and plants a seed. In a flash, an olive tree grows to its full height. There is no contest. The people have found their patron Goddess and the village will grow into the jewel among the city-states of ancient Greece—Athens, the city of Athena.

The Parthenon temple is built in her honour atop the Acropolis.

Athena is the Goddess of War. But is war only external? Is war only about fighting with 'others'? Who are these 'others'? The greatest war might well be the one we fight within ourselves—the war that our virtues wage upon our vices and, in turn, our vices wage upon our virtues.

Goddess Athena provides able stewardship in this battle. For, interestingly, she is also the Goddess of Wisdom. And of Justice, Courage, Arts and Civilization itself. She is the Goddess of Compassion and Refinement. She even invented the flute. No wonder she was the patron Goddess of the great city of Athens.

She is often depicted holding an owl in one hand. Sometimes, she is also depicted alongside an olive tree.

Nachiket: 'Madness. To wantonly destroy such beauty.'

Gargi: '*Parabalani*, they were called, *the reckless ones.* *Parabalani*—what an ironically musical word. They were militaries of the faithful, according to Nixey. They were controlled by clerics and moved in packs—swarms, actually. Sometimes of over 500 men. They attacked temples, idols, sacred groves ... they even entered the homes of pagans and seized all the idols and any books that seemed "ungodly" to them. They called them "demonic writings", according to Nixey.'

Anirban: 'Actually, the problem is fundamental. Such behaviour seems to be sanctioned in the Bible itself, in the Old Testament. In the Book of Deuteronomy[7], God commands his Chosen People to destroy the altars of the old Gods, tear down graven images, burn sacred groves. Anyway, the first commandment given to Moses on Mount Sinai is, "Thou shalt have no other Gods before Me." Deuteronomy says an idolator should be stoned to death. A pretty clear directive, huh?'

Dharma Raj: 'Human nature is the same everywhere. There are intolerant militant minds among all religions and communities. Doctrinal sanction embeds the problem more deeply.'

Gargi: 'In Palmyra,[8] they chopped off Goddess Athena's head, her arms and shoulders. All over the Roman empire, they tore down temples, smashed and disfigured statues.'

Lopamudra: 'Over 1,000 years later, the Islamic State militants did it once again in Palmyra. They brought Goddess Athena down too.'

Dharma Raj: 'But she had already been brought down, right, Gargi? Isn't that what your book says?'

Priding himself in knowing international history more than his friends, the well-travelled Anirban edged in. 'She had been rebuilt after that, Uncle. Painstakingly rebuilt.'

'Hello! Mr Know-It-All! Papa asked me,' Gargi snapped.

Anirban: 'Sorry.'

Gargi: 'Nixey writes about this second event also, Ma. That's what made me cry. I remember her words so clearly. "Once again, [Goddess] Athena was beheaded. Once again, her arm was sheared off." I don't think I'll ever forget these sentences. They're seared into my psyche.'

Nachiket: 'I love your hyperbole.'

'You love everything about her,' Dharma Raj quipped dryly.

Nachiket laughed.

4

JEALOUS FAITH
UNLEASHED

Lopamudra had once been a voracious reader of books. But now she read human beings—it was a secret indulgence she rarely discussed with anyone, although she suspected she had this in common with her husband. Someday they would reach this intimacy as well; maybe discuss each other like a well-read book.

She keenly observed her daughter and son-in-law now. Often, during a quiet moment, she wondered whether Nachiket was merely fond of his wife, without intensity or deep passion. What aspects of her did he respect? Were they partners—did she challenge him, did he challenge her? Or were they just each other's comfort zones? Must we be challenged by our partners? Gargi certainly amused him. And he, in turn, anchored her free and unrestrained spirit.

She banished her thoughts and dived back into the ongoing discussion.

Anirban: 'Goddess Athena was not the only one, Gargi. All the Gods and Goddesses—Goddess Aphrodite in Athens, Goddess Minerva in Germany, God Apollo in Italy—suffered brutally at the hands of men. The Serapis temple in Alexandria was torn down and the church of

John the Baptist was built over it. Many leaders among these destroyers were canonized. The church made them saints—Saint Martin, Saint John Chrysostom. Saint Benedict destroyed the Apollo temple in Italy, for instance.'

Nachiket: 'Amazing, the pitfalls of certainty. "I am right." "You are wrong." "I must destroy your way of life for your own good."'

Gargi: 'Worshipping the old Gods was forbidden by the law itself in many places. The old books were piled high in public squares and burnt.'

Nachiket: 'Madness. Pure madness.'

Anirban: 'Almost all ancient ways of life were reformatted and overwritten.'

Lopamudra: 'It was done to us as well—by the Turks and the Europeans.[9] The idols of our Gods and Goddesses were beheaded, temples destroyed, universities burnt to cinders because they contained "demonic books". These books were on a brand of spirituality that questioned and explored, and science that guided.'

Gargi: 'But, we did not get reformatted. The ancient Dharmic way—Hinduism, Jainism, Buddhism and, their youngest sibling, Sikhism—survived. It's still living and breathing. Our ancestors stubbornly kept rebuilding. They refused to give up their way of life. Historians say that the Somnath temple was rebuilt seventeen times. It was destroyed first by the Turk Mahmud Ghazni, although some historians say the Arab invader Al-Junayd was the first to desecrate it[10]. Our ancestors did not capitulate. Apostatize, I believe the word is. But many of our fellow travellers on the Paths of Ancient Wisdom, from Rome to Egypt, disappeared.'

Lopamudra: 'Yes. It's interesting though, that while there are so many examples of idol-rejecting cultures massacring idol-worshipping "others", there are no historical instances that I am aware of, of idol-worshipping cultures going around killing "others" simply because they did *not* worship idols. Nobody said: "I will kill you because you reject idols."'

Anirban: 'Not sure about this. There is evidence of Jain and Buddhist temples and statues being destroyed by Hindus.[11] And vice versa also, to be fair.'

Lopamudra: 'No denying that. But are you saying a few murders are equal to a genocide? There were attacks by some pagans on other pagans, but they were political moves. It was not because the Jain, Buddhist and Hindu scriptures called the "other" evil and mandated that they be annihilated. Christian and Islamic destruction of idolatry was also political, but the primary motive was doctrinal and religious. And this has been attested to by them, proudly, in their own recorded primary sources[12]... Thus, they were dramatically more extensive. According to their dogma, it was a noble mission to massacre idol-worshippers and destroy their temples; this was not just a play out of political ambitions and it added brutal zealotry to the politics. Idol-worshipping cultures did not wipe out other cultures *because* idols were not being worshipped; their doctrines did not support this extremism.'

Anirban: 'I accept what you are saying, Aunty. But what about the genocide of Jains and Buddhists in India?'

Lopamudra: 'Genocide?'

Anirban: 'Well, they are completely missing in India. Obviously then, they have suffered genocide I would say.'

Gargi: 'Wow! That's one hell of a leap!'

Anirban shrugged.

Lopamudra: 'Firstly, the Jains were always a small community. A very influential community to this day, but a small community ...'

Gargi: 'Nachiket and I were in Ranakpur *derasar* (a Jain temple in Ranakpur, Rajasthan) two months back. It was so peaceful, well organized, clean ... oh my God, so clean!'

Nachiket: 'She is not exaggerating this time. Honestly, it was so clean and calming. I want to take Ma and Papa there one day.'

Dharma Raj: 'I'd love to go, but we are digressing from the discussion. Go on, Lopa.'

Lopamudra: 'Moving on to Buddhists, in many parts of the Indian subcontinent where they were a substantial proportion of the local population—Afghanistan and parts of Pakistan, for instance—they were wiped out by Turkic invaders during the twelfth century.'

Dharma Raj: 'Is that true? Wiped out by the Turks, I mean … There could have been other reasons.'

Lopamudra: 'Dr Ambedkar has written about this in *Pakistan or the Partition of India*[13].'

Anirban nodded. 'Hmmm. Thank you for suggesting the book. Will definitely read it.'

Lopamudra continued: 'Furthermore, the Buddhists are still here, in India. In a very large proportion, if I may add.'

Anirban jumped in with renewed energy. He finally had figures to argue with. 'They are merely 0.7 per cent of the population, Aunty. Is that really a high proportion?'

Lopamudra smiled. 'I have this to say to you—you are using a colonial definition of what the religious composition of a country should be like. The West believes that you can practise only one religion, to the exclusion of all else. But that is not how pagans see the world, Anirban. Lord Gautam Buddha is worshipped as the ninth avatar of Lord Vishnu. Seen in this light, many Vaishnavs—followers of Lord Vishnu—are also Buddhists. That makes Buddhists around 10–15 per cent of the Indian population.'

Anirban: 'This is sophistry, Aunty. A clever but unacceptable argument. By the way, in South India, Lord Gautam Buddha is not seen as an avatar of Lord Vishnu.'

Lopamudra: 'Granted. It is a North Indian Vaishnav belief. That's why I counted the Buddhists as only 10–15 per cent of the population.'

Dharma Raj: 'Anirban, what Lopa is saying will appear as sophistry only to a Westernized mind because it thinks that only One God—and a male One at that—can be worshipped, and all else must be rejected as falsehood. That one can follow only one religion and reject all others. Japan is a pagan society that was not colonized, and Shintos are 70 per cent of the population. But Buddhists are 67 per cent! That makes the gross total far more than 100 per cent! Wrap your mind around those figures![14] This means most Japanese follow both Shintoism and Buddhism, which reflects in their modern data as well.'

Anirban: 'Wow! I did not know this. Very interesting.'

Lopamudra: 'In India, many "Hindus" follow Hinduism as well as Buddhist traditions. They worship Lord Buddha as an avatar of Lord Vishnu and are aware of the Four Noble Truths and the Eightfold Path. Many Hindus follow Jain traditions and practise vegetarianism. Many Jains visit Hindu temples and worship Lord Ganesh and Lord Shiva. You see a mirror image in Southeast Asia, where many Buddhists worship Lord Ganesh and celebrate the stories from the Mahabharata and Ramayana. There's another example that we all know but very few acknowledge. It is officially believed that

1.7 per cent of the Indian population is Sikh. But many Hindus keep images of Guru Nanak ji in their puja room. Many Sindhi and Punjabi Hindus keep the Guru Granth Sahib at home. They also pray in Sikh gurdwara as well as Hindu temples. So, are they Hindu or Sikh? Or both? We are not forced to pick one and reject the other.'

Anirban: 'Point taken, Aunty. I never looked at it this way.'

Nachiket: 'Further, an idol-worshipper is open-minded and humble when it comes to religion. If we are willing to worship anything, even a stone, then we shouldn't have a problem with those who worship differently. Pray to whoever you want, however you want. You can't be *wrong*. "I may be right but others may also be right", versus "*Only* I am right, all others are wrong and will burn in hell for eternity."'

Anirban: 'Okay. That, too, is an excellent point.'

Lopamudra: 'Idol-worshippers were also nature worshippers in the past. The hoary past, over two millennia ago, when this way of life flourished. They were the original environmentalists, though it would be hard to believe that today. They considered everything to be divine. Nature was not just created as a resource for our use, it was more like a Divine Parent to be worshipped.'

Anirban: 'Doesn't work like that in real life.'

Lopamudra laughed. She said, 'True, my dear sceptic. Human beings—our species—we are WIPs. Works in progress. But doctrine serves as a powerful lighthouse for most of us—certainly for most human communities. Doctrine and religious theory matter. It's the signpost.'

Anirban: 'Hmmm. So, Nature is like God.'

Nachiket: 'Nature is not *like* God. It *is* God, for pagan cultures. There's no difference.'

Gargi: 'Goddess, actually!'

Lopamudra: 'God and Goddess. Gods and Goddesses.'

Nachiket: 'Idol-worshipping, or *murti puja* as we call it, should not be a cause for embarrassment. Or intellectual coyness. It should be a matter of pride.'

Anirban raised his eyebrows. That was a vehement assertion from his laidback friend. He realized that Nachiket was an ardent murti pujak, albeit his other half, Gargi, was much more verbose. His opinions were quiet, in line with his comfort as a person. After all, Anirban mused, he had gone down on his knees and paid full obeisance to Lord Ganesh in the hospital as they had entered; Gargi had not.

Anirban persisted. 'I don't know. I get the political points—this is who we are, this is our identity and we may as well be comfortable in our skin. But philosophically, I don't get it. I love the stories, mind you, all of them— Egyptian, Greek, Roman, Mexican and Native American. Even our own stories about rishis and ancient kings ... but what are they? Honestly, are they history? Mythology? Real or make-believe? And what's the point of it all?'

Dharma Raj: 'The point depends on what you make of it. It is usually personal.'

Anirban raised his eyebrows again. 'What does that mean? Is faith personal?'

Gargi turned to her father: 'Yes, Papa. What do you mean by personal?'

Lopamudra: 'Okay, let me take this. To begin with, we are discussing much more than faith here, Anirban; a much larger space than faith. Of course, in that larger space we do not discard faith. But let us see idol worship as a symbolic unfolding. Let us try and build an open network of ideas.'

Dharma Raj: 'We are not seeking a logical progression. Symbolic language moves laterally. Anirban, you connect idols with faith. Heartfelt faith is *bhakti*. Nachiket is cast in that mould. For Gargi, it is intellectual, I suspect. Lopa and me ... we are trying to explore if idolatry can serve as a portal to self-discovery. I used the phrase "personal" in that sense.'

Anirban: 'So, no linear progression of ideas?'

Dharma Raj: 'That too ... let's explore together.'

Lopamudra: 'Okay, tell me, who's your favourite God or Goddess? Who are you inspired by?'

Gargi: 'I will go first. Please, please. Lord Krishna.'

Lopamudra: 'And yours, Nachiket?'

Gargi: 'Wait, I'm not done yet. Lord Shiva and Lord Ram.'

Nachiket: 'Lord Ganesh and Lord Hanuman.'

Lopamudra: 'Anirban?'

Anirban: 'Honestly, idol worship doesn't make sense to me. And yet, I must admit, I like our Lord Ganesh.'

Lopamudra: 'Okay. For me, it's Goddess Saraswati and Goddess Lakshmi. Papa says he's inspired by spiritual gurus like Sai Baba. And, of course, the formless, the Source of it all according to our Upanishads—the Brahman.'

Gargi: 'He's also partial to Lord Shiva. Aren't you, Papa?'

Dharma Raj's face softened as he looked at his daughter.

Anirban: 'Uncle, I wish I had your ability to allow your wife and daughter to speak for you without getting perturbed. I'm wondering if I should give that space to my wife sometimes. Or not.'

Gargi: 'I love this about Ma and Papa. They do not have prickly egos and their intimacy allows for this. Anyway, Papa easily gives emotional space to all and sundry to exercise proprietary ownership of him. Why not Ma?!'

Everyone laughed.

Anirban: 'I don't understand Brahman completely, Uncle. What is it? Everything? Then why the Gods and Goddesses? If you mention the unitary God—which is what Brahman is, to my understanding—then all these other Gods are merely subsets of the unitary God, the Brahman. Then the rest of the discussion becomes pointless. Isn't that so?'

Dharma Raj: 'Not to my way of looking at things. The connection between the one and the many is not a lived experience, often. It is a theoretical idea which has been expounded upon by many eminent thinkers, from Maharishi Yajnavalkya, Saptrishi Vashishtha to Roger Bacon and the theosophists. The message hasn't reached home to very many as yet. Certainly not to me. Experientially, we are all caught up in distinctness, polarization and separation. We are deeply prone to casting ourselves in opposition to some or the other "other". Let's try and avoid an "on the other hand" approach right now. As for the Brahman ...'

Brahman[15] is the macrocosmic reality. It is the truth, the only One Reality when stripped of *maya* (*illusion*). It has no form and can only be experienced. It is a consciousness that is expanding endlessly. It is eternal.

Brahman is One. All expressions, forms and beings are encompassed within it. It is the everything that we are all a part of. Our sense of separateness is an illusion.

The ultimate goal of life is to attain a consciousness of being that is part of the macrocosmos, of the unity of life—to know: if I am a proton, then *who* am I a constituent of? The atom! If I am an atom, then *who* am I a constituent of? The molecule—the DNA molecule! If I am a DNA molecule, then *who* am I a constituent of? The living cell! If I am a living cell, then *who* am I a constituent of? Maybe a lung! If I am a lung, then *who* am I a constituent of? Maybe a tiger! Or 'me'. Or 'you'. If I am a tiger, then *who* am I a constituent of? If I am 'me' or 'you', then *who* am I or you a constituent of? The One of whom all material life is the building block.

Space for intuition is created when the self-evident identity is questioned and logic is confounded.

All life is Brahman, the formless God. All forms—including Gods and Goddesses—can serve as stepping stones towards the formless God.

Lopamudra: 'Do you understand everything, Anirban?'

Anirban laughed ironically. 'All right. So, we all have personal preferences …'

Lopamudra: 'These are your *Ishta Devata*.'

Anirban: 'Meaning?'

Lopamudra: 'Your *Desired* or *Chosen God*. You get drawn to a deity, even if you don't really understand why. It's like falling in love or feeling an inexplicable pull.'

Anirban: 'I don't get it.'

Dharma Raj: 'The deity is like a mirror. It can resonate your emotions. You see what you want to see. You see *yourself* the way you want to see yourself. And if you enable yourself, you see what you need to see.'

Lopamudra smiled and shook her head. She met her husband's eyes in amusement. *Your legions of fans and admirers! Raj, the deity!*

Dharma Raj had a naughty glint in his eye.

Gargi: 'Ma, Papa, I really don't like the two of you sharing private jokes. You know I feel left out.'

Nachiket: 'Papa, please tell her what she wants to hear ...'

Dharma Raj: 'How can you be left out, Gargi? You're my centre.'

Nachiket smiled.

Gargi: 'Did the two of you just play me?!'

Dharma Raj laughed aloud. Nachiket's smile widened.

Lopamudra: 'Raj does this with everyone. He makes everyone feel special and included. I once outed him while he was talking to someone and he said to me, "Telling people what they want to hear calms them down. You may then find the opening to tell them what they need to hear ..."'

Gargi: 'That's Papa's expertise. Actually, Nachiket, you are like that too.'

Anirban: 'Getting back to this *Ishta Devata* business, everyone ... Why so many Gods and Goddesses? My chosen God. Your chosen Goddess ...'

Dharma Raj: 'Our personalities are very diverse, Anirban. No two individuals are exactly the same. And yet, we can broadly divide people into two categories— those who've awakened to an inner life and those who haven't. Different paths are available for solace and support. And then, self-understanding.'

Anirban: 'You've shifted the goalposts, Uncle. I thought we were discussing Gods and faith. But now you are speaking of self-understanding.'

Dharma Raj: 'Goalposts will shift. It's a network of ideas, like Aunty said. You again connected idol worship and idols to faith, Anirban. It can be a lot more. Faith is like first grade in school. We remain in school a lot longer.'

Gargi: 'And then once you finish school, there is college. If faith is first grade in school, then self-understanding is a post-graduate course?!'

Lopamudra: 'Yes, Gargi. But in the area of Dharma, you may find yourself studying in first grade and in college at the same time!'

Turning to Anirban, Lopamudra continued, 'Anirban, it does not matter whether you believe in Gods or Goddesses, or not. We are not making a case for or against, here. We are exploring something vast and complex which encompasses all life. Don't look for silo discussions in which we close one subject and then start another. There are different strands. Who knows, they may all lead to the same place. Look upon it as exploring something through the internet. You are reading an article, and you find an interesting sub-topic linked to a hyperlink, and then you click on that hyperlink, go to that sub-topic and study further. You will discover your own unique path through the internet. As will all of us.'

Anirban: 'I understand what you're saying. I am trying my best to understand every word you all are saying. But this is an unfolding.'

Gargi: 'It is …'

Lopamudra: 'It is a search. We are all groping in the dark, together. Tell me, do you think God is an external entity, someone "out there"? Or is God an inner experience?'

Anirban: 'I have often thought about it. The subject fascinates me, though I can't say I've got any great insights on it.'

Lopamudra: 'Nachiket, what do you think?'

Nachiket: 'Both?'

Dharma Raj laughed, 'Gargi, you've married an intuitive man. I don't think you fully understand what you've just said, Nachiket. But you're right. And on that note, Lopa, can I have another cup of tea?'

Lopamudra laughed: '*Do ghoont?*'

Dharma Raj gave her a thumbs up: 'Two sips!'

5

THE PRINCIPLES
OF PLEASURE

Tea in hand, Dharma Raj continued, 'The concept of Gods is very attractive to some people. In India we have various deities, and many are pulled towards them. There are others who may be spiritual but do not need any external anchoring. You know, the *Kathopanishad* mentions two interesting words: *Shreyas* and *Preyas*.'

Indian philosophy is anchored in the four Vedas: Rig Veda, Sama Veda, Atharva Veda and Yajur Veda. Each of them ends with philosophical musings, which in later years came to be known as Upanishads. They are also called *Vedanta*; the *end of the Vedas*.

Upanishad can be translated as 'sitting at the feet'. Disciples sat at the feet of their gurus who revealed the nature of Life and the Universe. Traditionally there are ten major ancient Upanishads, viz. Isha, Kena, Katha, Prashna, Munda, Mandukya, Taittiriya, Chandogya, Aitareya and Brihadaranyaka. Shvetashvatara, Kaushitaki and Maitrayani are other ancient Upanishads. The *Muktikopanishad* mentions as many as 108 Upanishads. Collating lists from different sources, this number can grow to several hundreds. These minor Upanishads can be divided into categories like Shaiva, Shakta, Vaishnava, Yoga, Sannyasa, Samanya, etc. They were passed down the ages orally till they were finally put in writing.

Dara Shikoh, the eldest son of Shah Jahan, translated many Upanishads from Sanskrit to Persian in the seventeenth century. He took the help of Pandits from Kashi (Banaras, now Varanasi, Uttar Pradesh, India) to aid him in this endeavour.

The *Kathopanishad* is one of the most well-known Upanishads and comes at the end of the Krishna Yajurveda. It is presented as a conversation between young Nachiket, an iconic disciple in Indian philosophy, and Yama, the Lord of Death.

Sage Vajashrava performed a ritual sacrifice to accumulate good karma. It required that he give away all his possessions, but Nachiket, his son, soon realized that his father was not giving *him* away. He too was dear to his father, and he repeatedly asked Vajashrava to also give him away. The sage lost his cool and told his son that he would give him to Lord Yama, the God of Death. This was received as an order by the earnest boy, and he approached Lord Yama, who was also known as *Dharma Raj,* the *Lord of Dharma*.

It led to a conversation between Nachiket and Dharma Raj that reverberates through millennia as the *Kathopanishad*.

Nachiket: '*Shreyas* and *Preyas*. Okaaay …?'

Dharma Raj: '*Preyas* means all that is pleasing to our senses.'

Nachiket: 'Hmmm … Gargi, I'm calling you "Preyas" from today!'

Everyone laughed.

Lopamudra: 'Because she's pleasing to you? Or because she's pleasure-seeking?'

Gargi: 'Both, I suppose!'

Nachiket: 'One thing my wife is never short of— honesty!'

Dharma Raj continued, 'What pleases the sense organs is momentary. And Nachiket, almost all human beings live in the world of *Preyas*. Not just your Gargi.'

Gargi nodded vigorously.

Lopamudra: '*Preyas* goes beyond pleasure actually. Even rationally, we rely on what our sense organs perceive. We pride ourselves on our empirical exactitude.'

Anirban shrugged. 'Can't be such a bad thing! And what is *Shreyas*?'

Dharma Raj: '*Shreyas* is Dharma. The correct. The balanced. It's also permanent bliss. But this bliss is rare. Only very few rishis and spiritual gurus know what it's like. And even they only wander in and out of this state. Let's try and roadmap *Shreyas* and *Preyas*.'

Anirban: 'Why not debate them first?'

Lopamudra: 'Because debates are oppositional. And because both *Shreyas* and *Preyas* are valid. There's no competition here. Also, because we experience what our nature allows us to experience. Not what it cannot ... It's silly to get into the debate of whether *Shreyas* is better or *Preyas*. Transformation is a personal journey and it requires customization. One size does not fit all.'

Dharma Raj: 'For instance, my wife rarely debates aggressively while my daughter only knows how to confront head on!'

Rishika Lopamudra[16] was a renowned philosopher and scholar in the Vedic era. She contributed to the writings in the Rig Veda and is also credited with the Panchadasi Vedanta mantra of the Shakta traditions. She is the wife of Rishi Agastya and also a rishika in her own right.

According to the legend, Rishi Agastya forged a perfect woman for himself. She was beautiful, inside and out. She had the wisdom of a philosopher and an intellect as sharp as a knife. She possessed an analytical mind and was compassionate. She was full of knowledge and yet possessed the curiosity of the keen disciple. She was poetic and prosaic, composed and animated. She could adopt the wiles of an enchantress and then befuddle the minds of intellectuals.

She dwells among us in her reincarnated form as the River Kaveri.

The *Brihadaranyaka Upanishad* tells us the story of the great Rishika Gargi. King Janak of Videha was a genteel philosopher-king. His assemblies of the learned were famous throughout the land of Bharat. Rishikas and rishis flocked to the kingdom to exercise their intellect and deepen their wisdom.

On one such occasion, he centred the debate on the esoteric subject of Brahman. The debate began and learned men and women came forth and bowed out quickly. Finally, there were two left: Rishi Yajnavalkya and Rishika Gargi.

She was eloquent and firm. She could not be cornered. She asked about the inner, unseen world of thoughts, energy and self-reflection, and swung to the outer world which is accessed through our sense organs—the first being the microcosm and the second, macrocosm.

Who won? We do not know. But does it matter? The debate was on the Many, the Dual, the One.

Gargi: 'Ma can give you a good run for your money, Papa, if you venture into world politics!'

Dharma Raj: 'True. She knows how to leave me speechless! But Anirban is itching to say something. What is it, young man?'

Anirban: 'Well, it seems we are back to self-understanding. Self-understanding through my attraction to Lord Ganesh?!'

Dharma Raj: 'You can reach it with or without Lord Ganesh. It depends on who you are.'

Nachiket: 'Or, what you are. For instance, I'm hungry. Should I order some dinner from the hotel? Masaale bhaat and alu?'

Gargi: 'Good idea! I'm hungry too and the discussion is getting too deep already. I'd like some vaangyache bharit with jwarichi bhakari also. And some thecha. And something gode (sweet).'

6

THE CONTEMPLATIVE PROCESS

The suite had a cosy antechamber where the group sat and ate. Later, they moved back to the main section along with sheera, their dessert.

Gargi: 'How was your day, by the way?'

Lopamudra: 'Hectic. We did a stress test on a treadmill. Papa's heart is stronger than mine. Not that mine is too bad, mind you. Lots of other tests throughout the day.'

Nachiket: 'Can we go home tomorrow?'

'Yes, you can. *Aaram se. (Easily.)*' Dr Adarsh Bhattacharya had quietly walked in. 'Hello everybody. *Thinava*, Anirban. Namaskar, Aunty and Uncle. I had to look in on a patient and decided to drop by.'

Dharma Raj: 'Superb. Join us. Would you like some dinner? Nachiket called for some excellent home-style food from his Ego Hotel. Funny name.'

Dr Adarsh: 'It is, isn't it? No, thank you. I'll wait till I get home.'

Lopamudra got up and walked to the antechamber. 'Well, you must have some sheera, then. No choice. *Basa. (Sit.)*'

Dr Adarsh obediently took a seat. Lopamudra walked back and handed him a bowl. He dug into the generous helping of sheera.

Anirban: 'Join us if you have some time, Adarsh. We're having an interesting conversation. You will enjoy it.'

Dr Adarsh: 'What are you talking about?'

Anirban: 'Idol worship.'

Dr Adarsh: 'Wow! My wife and I have just returned from Pashupatinath ji temple in Kathmandu. Very powerful vibes. Which deity were you discussing?'

'Right now, it's *Shreyas* and *Preyas*!' Nachiket chuckled.

'Okay.' Adarsh frowned in confusion.

Gargi: 'Actually we're building a case for idol worship.'

Dr Adarsh: 'Building a case? Why, what's the problem?'

Anirban: 'Are you comfortable with idol worship?'

Dr Adarsh: 'Aren't we all? My daughter, Payal, has just sculpted a clay Lord Ganesh idol for the day after tomorrow. Eco-friendly. Let me show you a picture.'

He fiddled with his phone and passed it around.

Lopamudra: 'She's five years old now, isn't she?'

'Yes, already. How time flies!' Dr Adarsh said, as he put the phone back in his shirt pocket.

Anirban: 'What does idol worship mean to you, Adarsh?'

Dr Adarsh: 'Haven't really given it a thought. *Khoob bhalo laage. (It feels nice.)* I guess it's grounded in the idea that the divine exists in everything. And everyone. If I can see the divine in a stone, then why not in Nature? A human being? Even my enemy?'

Anirban: 'Does it happen, though? Or does it just lead to superstition and exploitation?'

Dr Adarsh: 'Everything is open to exploitation and misuse. Razor blades can be misused! Should we get rid of them then? Even modern medicine can be exploited. Josef Mengele was an accomplished doctor. But what a monster!'

Dharma Raj: 'I like that. The razor blade too has other possibilities! If understood, that is.'

Dr Adarsh: '*Shreyas* and *Preyas*. That's the good and pleasure. But how does this connect to idol worship?'

Lopamudra: 'We'll get to idol worship in good time. Be patient!'

Dr Adarsh: 'Okay. Uncle?'

Dharma Raj: 'So, Dharmic religions seek harmony and balance in two directions: the external world, which is accessible to us through our sense organs, and our inner world, which is accessible to us through reflection and meditation. The world of action and the world of observation. Let me mention two other words: *Nivrutti* and *Pravrutti*. The *Nivruttic* and *Pravruttic* impulses.'

Nachiket: 'Which one should I pick between the two?'

Lopamudra: 'You pick what you can. You would be almost blind to the other.'

Anirban: 'What do they mean?'

Dharma Raj: 'Actually, Rajiv Malhotra calls them the Sanskrit non-translatables,[17] and with good reason. But loosely speaking, *Nivrutti* is the act of halting, returning. It's moving away from the five senses and turning our attention within.'

Gargi: 'And *Pravrutti* is for those who live in the world of *Preyas*, I suppose?'

Dharma Raj: 'Yes, but more. *Pravrutti* is to proceed; to move towards the world of the senses.'

Dr Adarsh: 'Fascinated as I am, I'm still a little lost. How does this connect with *Shreyas* and *Preyas*?'

Lopamudra: 'Stay with *Nivrutti* and *Pravrutti* for now. The point is that we can explore in either direction. *Nivrutti* is contemplative; its tool is meditation. God is "*nirguna niraakaar*", *without qualities and form*.'

Dharma Raj: 'And *Pravruttic* people live in the world of senses. It is "real" to us, but it is a storehouse of perception of poorly or not-poorly kept records. This is the only "reality" many people know. But they too can be seekers.'

Nachiket: 'What is the tool for *Pravrutti*?'

Lopamudra: 'Prayer and worship.'

Nachiket: 'And idol-worshipping is for *Pravruttic* people?'

Anirban: 'Okay. I take that. But why did you mention self-understanding, Uncle? How does that happen?'

Lopamudra: 'Self-understanding happens only obliquely, if at all. Solace is good enough.'

Dharma Raj: 'Nobody worships with the goal being self-understanding.'

Anirban: 'I should imagine so! Can we discuss the *Nivruttic* path first? I find it more interesting. It's the internal path, so I suppose Godhood would be internal. And *Pravrutti* is the external path; God, or Gods, are external.'

Dharma Raj: 'Internal life has begun for *Nivruttic* people. For others, life is external ...'

Lopamudra: 'How do we make this easy to understand? Can we ballpark some basic principles for both?'

Dharma Raj: 'Hmmm. Let us outline three pillar principles for both. First, *Nivrutti*. Lopa, why don't you take a shot?'

Lopamudra: 'Okay. The first would be *sthita prajna*. Then, *aatmabodha*. And the third ... I don't know. Tell me.'

Dharma Raj: 'I agree with the first two. The third, I would say, would be *karmaṇy-evādhikāras te mā phaleṣhu kadāchana*[18]... in short, *nishkaama karma*.'

Lopamudra: 'Aah ... Beautiful ...'

Gargi: 'Do you mind, you two? Explain to us, the morons.'

Dharma Raj smiled. '*Sthita prajna* is the still mind.' He glanced at his daughter, 'Something you do not possess, despite your Yoga expertise!'

Gargi scowled. Her father smiled and continued, 'Think of a monkey and a lion. What's the difference?'

Gargi: 'A monkey is always distracted; all over the place. The famous saying is that the monkey mind is the chattering mind. Aimless. But a lion walks with nobility, I suppose. Majestic and with a sense of purpose.'

Anirban: 'Hmmm … the lion. This reminds me of a homeless person who sits outside my gym in Mumbai. He's quite a guy—doesn't ask anybody for anything; just sits quietly. Like a lion, I suppose! Makes a dignified enquiry with his eyes. Malivalaya—my wife—gifted this homeless guy a portable music player. Now he sits with his eyes closed, listening to music. On the other hand, there are people who come to the gym throughout the day. I watch them sometimes; it's interesting. If the valet doesn't appear for half a minute, they get upset. Honk! Honk! Honnnnk! I guess, they are like the monkeys?! Their time is precious, after all.'

Gargi: 'On a side note, we call his wife Valli, incidentally. But he always uses her full name— Malivalaya. Everyone else calls her Valli! Do you do that in private too, Anirban? Ma-li-va-la-ya? Always?'

Anirban smiled enigmatically but did not reply.

Lopamudra: 'Your wife is Thai, isn't she?'

Anirban: 'Half-Thai, half-Sikh.'

Lopamudra: 'Hmmm … I'd love to meet her someday. Digressing a bit, but Gargi, I must say this. You're always fidgety in a queue.'

Gargi protested: 'ALWAYS?'

Lopamudra: 'Okay, not always in your body movements. But clearly always in your mind!'

Dharma Raj: 'Come on, Lopa. That's not fair! You've seen much worse. What about that cousin of yours? I remember the way she behaved in the restaurant the other day!'

Gargi: 'Aamodini Mashi?'

Lopamudra laughed. She said: 'Who else? Yes. The waiter dropped a spoon on the table. She raised her brows at him. That made the poor man so nervous that he spilled the palak paneer on the table while serving. She snapped immediately.'

Dharma Raj: 'Correction. She lost it. Started yelling like a banshee.'

Lopamudra: 'That's true. Monkey mind. No lion-walk for sure. Aamodini may be sophisticated in appearance, but her mind is always all over the place. That homeless boy of yours, Anirban … he's walking through life like a lion; some would say he's living the human experience in a far more fulfilled manner. Aamodini's mind is *asthir* (*restless*).'

Gargi: 'Ma is right about me, Papa. I should learn to be calm. I'll be able to handle life better. It's only when the mind is not chattering that one doesn't miss a detail. I must learn this.'

Nachiket: 'Wow! Self-understanding has begun!'

Gargi: 'Only in theory, okay? So, chill.'

Lopamudra smiled. 'Actually, *aatmabodha*, the second principle, is *self-understanding*. *Sthita prajna* is just the still mind or *steady wisdom*. Lord Krishna describes it beautifully in the Bhagavad Gita.[19] I'll show you when you come home. Raj, is it okay with you if I try and explain *aatmabodha*?'

Dharma Raj: 'I'm keenly listening, *Ardhaangini ji* (*wife*)!'

Lopamudra gently touched her husband's arm. 'So, *aatmabodha* may mean *self-understanding* but the English language does grave injustice to this word. It's more than a mere visit to the psychiatrist!'

Nachiket: 'Or your spouse, in which case the enlightenment is free of charge!'

Lopamudra: 'And therefore, discounted! No, it's not about decoding the personality. It's the realization that I'm *not* the personality; I am not my body, my emotions, my thoughts, my energies. The Bhagavad Gita tells us these are the clothes we wear[20], while we can be the still soul that observes. Even if I'm thinking intensely, I can be still. Even if my emotions are pouring out, I can be a step removed. Even if my body is in pain, I can place myself above the experience. My true nature is *Sat*, *Chit* and *Ananda*: *truth*, *consciousness* and *bliss*.'

Dharma Raj: 'And I must not just know this intellectually. I must, at some stage, experience it.'

Anirban: 'Is that possible for anyone?'

Lopamudra: 'I know I have not experienced it. But only in this state can we fully identify our *gunas* and *varnas*, the *shades* and *colours* of our temperament. Only then will I know that *I* do not suffer. Ever.'

Nachiket: 'You really need to explain this, Ma. What do you mean by "I do not suffer. Ever."?'

Lopamudra: 'Most people understand the difference between pleasure and happiness. Yes?'

Anirban: 'Hmmm …'

Lopamudra: 'The challenge lies in separating pain from suffering. Some people have a high pain threshold, others have a low pain threshold. Like Papa has a very high pain threshold. But what is a pain threshold? Does it mean that you are not feeling the pain till you reach your threshold? Of course, you are. Your body was experiencing the pain before. Reaching the threshold just means that now the experience of pain is distressing you.'

Nachiket: 'It is something like, "I'm miserable. I've lost my positivity now."'

Lopamudra: 'Yes. That's when you suffer. Till you reach this point, you are registering the pain but you're not allowing it to make you unhappy. You're okay.'

Dharma Raj: 'But this grit-your-teeth-and-be-positive ability is not really *aatmabodha*, is it?'

Lopamudra: 'No. It is strength, but it is not detachment from pain. *Aatmabodha* is not about having a high pain threshold but knowing that *you* are not in pain. Your body is in pain. Then you will have no threshold. Because you will not *factor in* the pain. You will not *suffer*, because of the pain.'

Gargi: 'Not even an "ouch"?'

Dharma Raj: 'Always make allowance for the "ouch"! It's de-pressuring. Let off steam. Just don't lose your deepest steadiness. Your body and emotions experience life. But you're an observer.'

Dr Adarsh: 'You are not in pain; your body is in pain. You are not thinking; your mind is thinking. You are not loving. Your heart is loving. You're a witness.'

Nachiket: '*Khup* theoretical *aahe.* (*It is very theoretical.*) Is it even possible?'

Dr Adarsh: 'Practise can only happen when the theory is understood well. And understanding the theory itself can take a lifetime. Huh, Uncle?'

Dharma Raj smiled.

Gargi: 'I'm leaving the practise for the next life!'

Dharma Raj: 'Aren't we all? One very practical thing I need to do right now is visit the washroom.'

Lopamudra: 'I'll call Mama.'

Gargi: 'Who's Mama?'

Lopamudra: 'The ward boy. He's called Mama. Come everyone, it's been a tiring day. Papa needs assistance.'

Lopamudra rang the bell as the others got up and left the room.

7

KNOW THYSELF;
KNOW THY DIVINE

Lopamudra peeped out of the room and asked the young people to come back in. They sat in the same places as before.

Anirban: 'Uncle, what about the third principle? It's the one that's well known.'

Lopamudra: 'I'm not done with *aatmabodha*.'

Anirban: 'Oops. I'm sorry!'

Lopamudra: 'Like I was saying, we should know what to factor in and what not to factor in. If your heart is feeling love, you factor in this love. If your mind is thinking a thought, and it's a good thought, then you factor it in. If your body is feeling pain; try to factor it in less as a feeling and more as a clue to what's going on in your body.'

Anirban: 'What does that mean?

Lopamudra: 'Okay. Picture yourself as swimming above your personality, as an observer. You dip into the experience, and then rise above the water and observe, learn, absorb the learning, discard the debris.'

Dharma Raj: '*Aatmabodha* is the insight that I am not Dharma Raj. Dharma Raj is an aspect of me, it's my machinery. I can tweak it as I deem fit. It is also the insight that Lopamudra, Adarsh, Anirban, Gargi and Nachiket are also my aspects. And I am their aspect. As are the trees, stars, animals, sun and moon. In union, there is no "othering".'

Lopamudra: 'Even your neighbour Bhide? Is he a part of your aspect too, Raj?!'

Dharma Raj chuckled. 'Can I leave him out? But you're right, Lopa. I get your point!'

Nachiket: 'If I have a sense of "other", I do not really understand. I do not have bodha of this atma! I do not know me. Ha!'

Dr Adarsh: 'Then I'm not really ready for *Nivrutti*; I must explore *Pravrutti* further. Hmmm?'

Dharma Raj: 'That's right. You think you understand but it's only intellectual understanding. You don't feel it. You don't become it. *Pravrutti* helps us to understand by experiencing. Feeling. And idols help in this understanding-through-feeling.'

Anirban: 'Before exploring *Pravrutti*, can we have the third principle of *Nivrutti*, Uncle?'

Dharma Raj: 'Aah! *Karmaṇy-evādhikāras te mā phaleṣhu kadāchana Mā karma-phala-hetur bhūr mā te saṅgo stvakarmaṇi.*[21] You see, *aatmabodha* cannot be an excuse for inaction and laziness. It is the foundation for *nishkaam karma, desireless* or *self-less action.*'

Karmaṇy-evādhikāras te mā phaleṣhu kadāchana Mā karma-phala-hetur bhūr mā te saṅgo stvakarmaṇi
Arguably, this is the most well-known shloka from the *Song of God.*[22]

Bhagavad Gita. Chapter 2, verse 47.

Krishna Dwaipayana is the son of Sage Parasara and Satyavati, a fisherwoman. We know him as Veda Vyasa, the compiler of the Vedas. Vyasa classifies the Vedas into four books: Rig, Yajur, Sama and Atharva. But the Vedas were difficult to understand. So, Vyasa decides to write a story which would serve as a metaphorical vehicle to convey the message of the Vedas to the people.

Lord Ganesh offers to become the narrator's scribe. But the Lord lays a condition: Vyasa cannot halt his narration. The narrator too has a condition: the quill of the writer cannot pause, even as the Lord must write only if it makes sense to Him.

The result of their joint effort: the Mahabharata, the grand epic from India.

The Mahabharata has eighteen chapters called parvas. The sixth chapter is the Bhishma Parva, or Book of Bhishma. It covers the first ten days of the Kurukshetra battle. Within the Bhishma Parva is the pearl of wisdom from India: Bhagavad Gita.

The Gita has eighteen sections which comprise sub-chapters twenty-three to forty of the Bhishma Parva.

The *Song of God* is a conversation between *Partha,* the friend and his *Saarthy* the guide; or Arjuna the Warrior and Lord Krishna the Charioteer.

Lopamudra: 'Yes. *Aatmabodha* is the foundation for *nishkaam karma*. Self-observation does not mean we disengage from life. We must observe and understand our psychology and be active at the same time. We must separate our actions from our internal pulls and emotions, and do what must be done.'

Gargi: 'How?'

Dharma Raj: 'By differentiating reaction from response. Reaction is instant and is triggered automatically by a stimulus from outside. Response is the result of reflection and is more conscious. We react to events all the time. In fact, we have a set list of reactions, depending on our personality. Even relationships develop set patterns. If someone insults me, I'll insult them. If someone is kind to me, I will be kind to them. If someone dislikes me, I will dislike them too. If this happens, I will do that, and so on. These are habits, prejudices and preconceived notions. It's our baggage. We often discount even a sensible input from a person we dislike, just because we do not like the source from whom the input is coming, even if it appeals to our senses. Instead, we must learn to respond. Reaction is immediate. Response is centred. So, it implies a time gap. Even silence is a response.'

Lopamudra: 'Basically, don't let others control your strings. Don't get triggered.'

Nachiket: 'Reminds me of a Lord Buddha story ...'

Siddhartha Gautama, the budding Lord Buddha, would wander as a sadhu and beg for alms. One day the mendicant knocks on a door and holds out his bowl when it opens. The man of the house is in a bad mood. He instantly begins to shout, 'You good-for-nothing! Why don't you work? Going around collecting freebies! Lazy! Lazy!' Siddhartha smiles, turns and leaves. This infuriates the man further. He runs after him and seizes his shoulder. 'I abuse you and you just walk off. What are you trying to prove?'

The mendicant replies, 'Suppose you had two oranges, and you offered them to me. But I declined to accept. What would happen to those two oranges?'

The man says, 'They would remain with me.'

The Lord Buddha gives his message, 'So it is with your abuse.'[23]

Lopamudra: 'Famous story, and still so true and relevant. The person who abuses you wants to hurt you, and you give them victory by getting hurt. Your reaction would be to hurt them as well. What a negative sum game! If you do not accept it, the transaction is not complete. It will remain with the giver then, and not have the power to hurt you. Accept the positive, and don't accept the negative.'

Nachiket: 'Otherwise you're a chattering monkey. Throw a pebble at a monkey. He throws it back at you. Throw a banana. He lunges for it. Throw another banana. He grabs it with the other hand. Throw another one ...'

Anirban: 'He drops one to catch this one. Throw two more. He drops everything ...'

Nachiket: 'Exactly! You throw a pebble at a lion. It may not react at all, if it's not in the mood! And if it's in the mood ... you know what will happen! The lion responds. Could it be mindful? With awareness? Who knows?!'

Anirban: 'I understand that you are making a humorous observation here, Nachiket, but earlier the lion was used as an example to show the grace of response. Here it seems to draw a line between animals and humans.'

Gargi: 'Well, Anirban, earlier the lion example was used as a metaphor to explain an idea, and now Nachiket is using that drawn line to crack a joke. Or, would you like to throw a pebble at a lion and see the reaction for yourself?'

Nachiket laughed while Anirban threw up his hands.

Lopamudra: 'Anyway, in our case, it must be so; responses being mindful and with awareness, that is. We must work towards it. We must ultimately become masters of our thoughts, feelings and actions. Understanding this is the first step. Happiness—or unhappiness—is not absorbed from the outside into us. We're not helpless. We must understand that events and people do not make us unhappy. Our unexamined perceptions do.'

Gargi: 'And our reactions to our own desires and sufferings. If you're looking for a reason to be happy, then you don't understand what happiness is.'

Anirban: 'Lao Tzu's idea of *wei wu wei*, which means *doing without doing*. If we break the chains of anxiety and desire, our actions become an end in themselves. Agenda-less actions. If you hope for an outcome, funnily you're working against that very outcome.'

Dr Adarsh: 'That's it. Agenda-less actions. *Karmaṇy-evādhikāras te* … It gives you focus. Otherwise, you may overlook a detail. This way you can do everything that needs to be done in the best way possible. And then be equanimous. You will probably get that result.'

Gargi straightened her back. 'Are we done with the inner world? I don't think I'm ready for it. Someday …'

Nachiket: 'Next life?'

Gargi grimaced. 'Probably. You better be there! Right now, only this outer world is real to me. Despite my Yoga!'

Lopamudra: 'You don't practise Yoga, like I've told you multiple times! What you do practise is Ashtanga Yogasana.'

Anirban: 'What's the difference?'

Nachiket and Gargi responded in chorus, 'Some other day ...'

Yoga is union. To join in harmony.

It is the joining of individual consciousness—the microcosm—with universal consciousness—the macrocosm. It is also the union inside us—of aligning our self-talk and emotions with our words and behaviour and, thus, attaining internal balance and harmony.

Rishi Patanjali[24] codifies an eight-fold path to this grand union in the Yoga Sutras and calls it *Ashtanga Yoga*, the *eight limbs of Yoga*:

1. Yama: self-restraint

2. Niyama: self-observances

3. Asana: physical postures

4. Pranayama: breathing

5. Pratyahara: withdrawing from the sensual

6. Dharana: concentration

7. Dhyana: meditation

8. Samadhi: uniting with the whole; pure consciousness

Asana, pranayama and pratyahara help us to dissociate our consciousness from the outside environment.

Rishi Patanjali defines yogasana as *sthiram sukham aasanam*, which means *the steady and comfortable posture*. It is the ability to sit in comfort for an extended period, which is a prerequisite for pranayama, dharana, dhyana and samadhi. Yogasana, then, is one of the eight. With it we gain the ability to set aside the body and not be distracted by it. To separate the body from the mind, so that it does not divert our attention.

Many asanas mimic the postures and movements of animals and creatures that live in greater harmony with both their environment and bodies. They understand harmony better than us.

Yogasana can align our energy channels and psychic centres. It can balance our autonomous nervous system and endocrinal system, our neurotransmitters and hormones.

Thus, yogasana prepares us for yoga.

Anirban: 'Okay, let's move to the world of sense organs. The outside world.'

Lopamudra: 'It is also the realm of the ego. But we need to get to the Gods and Goddesses soon. For Adarsh's sake.'

Dr Adarsh: 'I need to get home, actually. But I don't want to miss this.'

Nachiket: 'Papa, maybe you can name the three principles of *Pravrutti* and then we can call it a day.'

Dharma Raj: 'Okay. So, to begin with, *Pravrutti* is the life of perception through our senses. This is the world of fears, ambitions and desires.'

Lopamudra: 'Anger, passion, delight, suffering ... Satisfactions and dissatisfactions.'

Dharma Raj: 'It's the world we live in, and by default it comprises what we see, hear, touch, smell and taste.'

Anirban: 'Haven't the people in this room moved beyond survival? One where our basic needs are met?'

Dharma Raj: 'No, the basic needs have become more sophisticated and amplified. Subtle. We redefine basic, without realizing it. Need for food has become the need for good food, new food, exotic food, healthy food. Nachiket and Gargi travelled to Lucknow just for biryani.'

Gargi shrugged.

Lopamudra: 'Raj, you really nailed it, didn't you? Need for shelter becomes need for a bigger house, a fancy locality, a prettier house, a house with more rooms. Need for clothes is a big one! Huh, Gargi? More clothes, more colours, more patterns—that one's for me too!'

Gargi: 'Totally. Your exquisite saris!!'

Dharma Raj: 'I love her saris!'

Lopamudra: 'Aristotle's lollipop!'

Nachiket and Gargi laughed.

Anirban: 'Aristotle's lollipop? Meaning?'

Gargi: 'Ma teases Papa with this.'

Lopamudra: 'He's my sensual philosopher—attached and detached.'

Dharma Raj smiled. 'Philosophy without sensuality is food without salt. A palace without a door. Words without melody ...'

Lopamudra: 'Okay, okay. We get the point!'

Dharma Raj: 'Seriously though, the world of the senses is the world of survival. Competition. Economics. Money.'

Anirban: 'And what are the key spiritual signposts for this path? The principles?'

Dharma Raj: 'Lopa?'

Lopamudra: 'Your turn.'

Dharma Raj: 'I've given it some thought. *Ekam sat vipra bahudha vadanti* would be my first. Second is a compound of *Aham brahmasmi* and *Tat tvam asi*. And the third would be *Ishaavasyam idam sarvam. Yatkincha jagatyaam jagat ...*'

Gargi: 'Papa, we need a fresh mind for this. Let's shut shop for today.'

Dr Adarsh: 'Yes, my wife has been sending me crazy messages. I must run.'

Nachiket: 'Do you want me to drop the two of you home tomorrow, before I go to work? I could get here first thing in the morning.'

Lopamudra: 'I think we'll manage on our own. Come over in the evening, Anirban. Adarsh, join us. Maybe we can all have dinner together?'

Dr Adarsh: 'I won't stay for dinner. The day after is Ganesh Chaturthi, and there are still preparations left. But yes, I can come in the evening. 5.30?'

Anirban: 'What about your OPD?'

Dr Adarsh: 'I'll give it a break tomorrow. Move beyond survival for one evening!'

Nachiket: 'On that note, let's call it a day.'

The young people touched the feet of the two elders and filed out of the room, their minds buzzing with information and excitement.

8

ACCEPTANCE OF ALL; NO DISCRIMINATION

Gargi finished her yoga sessions and headed to her parents' home. Lopamudra and Dharma Raj had reached home by 10 a.m. It was a pleasant, fairly cool though humid day in Pune. Mother and daughter had a special task lined up for the day—a visit to Tulashi Baug to bring Ganpati Bappa home. Ten days earlier, on Janamashtami, Lopamudra had placed an order for an *eco-friendly idol*—a *shaduchi murti*—made from water-soluble clay found on the riverbanks.

They first headed to Ravivar Peth. Lopamudra bought the decorations for Ganpati Bappa from her favourite shop there. Her relationship with the shopkeepers had been fostered over thirty-five years.

After shopping, the mother–daughter duo decided to have lunch and then pick up the Lord's idol and head home. Carrying their shopping bags, they headed to Vadeshwar Restaurant on FC Road.

Gargi: 'This is the first time I will bring Bappa home with you, Ma. I have always accompanied Papa for this task.'

Lopamudra: 'Well, traditionally, Bappa should be brought home by the man of the house. Or else, the youngest boy in the family. But I decided that we best let Papa rest at home. We can bend such rules sometimes, hmmm?'

Gargi: 'It is completely all right with me. I'm enjoying doing this with you.'

They placed their orders. Lopamudra ordered bhajanicha thali peeth and dahi along with a mastaani mango milkshake. Gargi ordered their special sprouted moong salad chaat, a soya grilled sandwich and a chocolate protein shake.

Lopamudra: 'Gargi, I've been meaning to tell you for so long now. The thing is … please don't judge Nachiket.'

Gargi: 'Ma, I don't judge him. I love him.'

Lopamudra: 'Of course you do.'

Gargi: 'What? Judge? Or love?'

Lopamudra smiled: 'Both.'

Gargi: 'I wish he'd get a handle on his anger, that's all. He has these outbursts and then, later, blames himself for having lost control. He hurts himself by doing so. He physically hurts himself too, Ma. He puts himself out so much for other people. And then he snaps easily. Forever helping, forever assuaging. Forever there, for too many. He's crazy.'

Lopamudra: 'So, he doesn't set boundaries and then people make him in charge of their happiness. Even their well-being. Sounds like your Papa to me. He used to be like that. He still is, actually. The only difference is that earlier it used to deplete him, now he handles it better. He too has his share of *Shivji ki baraat*, like Lord Shiva did—the motley bunch of all types and kinds.'

Lord Shiva marries Goddess Parvati on Mahashivaratri, the Great Night of Lord Shiva.[25]

On the day of their wedding, Lord Shiva arrives at the doorstep of His father-in-law, Himavan, leading His band of followers. It is a motley crowd of Gods and demons, ghosts and vampires, animals, insects, reptiles and, what humans call, pests. Humans and non-humans. Big and small. Formed, deformed and semi-formed. These are His *gana*. None are excluded. No one is barred.

They do not necessarily like one another. They do not agree with each other, but tonight they have come together, for one thing that unites them all—their love for their Mahadev (the God of Gods), their Pashupatinath (Lord of the animals).

Himavan, king of the Himalaya mountains, is embarrassed, even outraged. Goddess Parvati's mother, Meena, faints and is unable to process the dire prospects for her precious daughter. Bewildered though the bride is, by the many bizarre creatures who accompany Her future husband, She accepts Him and them. Her lord is the Lord of all; He embraces all. No discrimination. No exclusion.

It is commonly believed that Lord Shiva marries Goddess Parvati on Mahashivaratri, which is celebrated on Krishna Paksha Chaturdashi—the fourteenth day of the waning moon—in the Hindu month of Phalgun in North India and Magha in South India. Remember, North India follows the Purnimanta calendar and South India follows the Amavasyanta calendar. North India, therefore, enters a new month a fortnight earlier. But the beauty of the 'unity in diversity' of India is that while the names of the months may differ, the day when North Indians and South Indians celebrate Mahashivaratri is exactly the same, and it usually falls in the Gregorian months of February or March.

Gargi: 'No wonder they get along so well, Papa and Nachiket.'

Lopamudra remained silent.

Gargi: 'I call them "his crazies". Seen it countless times, Ma. On the phone, listening, and then talking as if they are the most important people in his life. After hanging up though, he will chuck his phone and smash it to smithereens, screaming, "Why don't they leave me alone?" I just don't get it. I don't get his need to be there for these needy people. Can't he just tell them to lay off? How difficult can that be?'

Lopamudra: 'Gargi, let him be. That's who he is. We don't get to love a person and then reject one part of him. When you express your disapproval, it hurts him. That's all I'm saying.'

Gargi: 'I just withdraw, Ma. I wait for my wonderful man to re-emerge. That's easier—and he invariably does.'

Lopamudra: 'Okay. Good.'

Gargi and Lopamudra left the restaurant, and picked up the idol before finally heading home.

They reached home by 4.30 in the evening, tired but happy. Dharma Raj was in the kitchen, brewing his special ginger tea. The women had a quick shower and joined him in the veranda.

Gargi: 'Ma, do you want me to order some snacks for the evening? I suggest we just do the coffee and tea at home.'

Lopamudra: 'Good idea.'

Gargi: 'I'll call Nachiket and tell him to pick up some stuff.'

Lopamudra: 'That's the way you order the snacks?'

Gargi smiled.

Dharma Raj: 'I'd like some samosas. And kaande pohe. Let's indulge the *Pravruttic* impulse.'

Gargi: 'I don't think so, Papa. Only kaande pohe for you. Maybe I'll order idli instead of samosas. You can have them too.'

Dharma Raj: 'Lopa, your daughter is a bully.'

Lopamudra: 'So, she is my daughter now, is she? She is right, you know that. Papa won't have the samosas, Gargi. Don't worry. Order them for yourselves. Anirban will enjoy them. But yes, order idlis as well.'

Dharma Raj: 'Lopa, have you arranged a bhattji for the *puja* tomorrow?'

Lopamudra shook her head. 'Obviously not. I was waiting for you to remind me. Yes, I have, my good man. And for your information, it's a female bhattji.'

Gargi: 'Wow. That's wonderful.'

Dharma Raj: 'That's immaterial. She should be competent and sincere. *Tevadhe purey.* (*That's enough.*)'

Gargi: 'Optics matter, Papa.'

Dharma Raj: 'Whatever you say, raaja.'

Nachiket and Anirban rode in. Anirban got off the bike as Nachiket parked it under the neem tree.

Dharma Raj: 'Where's the good doctor?'

Anirban: 'On his way.'

Gargi: 'And where's the food?'

Nachiket: 'On its way. Why don't we sit in the garden? I'll bring out the chairs.'

Gargi: 'I'll get some more chai. And I'll inform Ma.'

Fifteen minutes later, as the small group settled down in their chairs near the tulsi hedge, Dr Adarsh Bhattacharya walked in.

Dharma Raj: 'Adarsh, would you like to park your car in the compound?'

Dr Adarsh: 'No, that's all right. I've parked it outside.'

Gargi: 'Would you like to freshen up?'

Dr Adarsh: 'No, thank you. I'm fine.'

Gargi: 'Some tea?'

Dr Adarsh: 'That'll be nice. *Aabhar.* (*Thanks.*) Anirban, are you all set for tomorrow?'

Lopamudra: 'Which mandal are you shooting at?'

Anirban: 'You will know tomorrow, Aunty. It's for a Bollywood biggie who wants to be photographed while he's visiting one of the *maanaache Ganpatis.*'

Gargi: 'Who is coming?' She handed a teacup to Dr Adarsh.

Anirban: 'You'll know tomorrow—it will make the news, I am sure.'

Gargi: 'Ma and I went shopping today. We brought Bappa home.'

Nachiket smiled. 'You broke the tradition, Ma. The women brought Bappa home, instead of the man of the house.'

Lopamudra: 'Yes, we did.'

Gargi: 'And, we have a female bhattji tomorrow. I approve!'

Dr Adarsh: 'Why not? Flexi-traditions, as my wife calls them. My daughter Payal and I made a Lord Ganesh idol at home. We used clay and toothpicks. She insisted that we use non-toxic colours to decorate it. I enjoyed it thoroughly.'

Lopamudra: 'How nice!'

Gargi: 'I hope the food does not take too long, Nachiket. I'm hungry.'

Nachiket: 'It'll be here soon. Idli, samosas and kaande pohe.'

Dr Adarsh: 'Samosas for Uncle?'

Dharma Raj: 'It's all maya, Adarsh!'

Everyone laughed.

Dharma Raj: 'Don't worry. I won't touch the stuff.'

Anirban: 'Maya is a good place to shift the gear back to the discussion this evening, I'm thinking. I've never understood this "maya" business. How is it possible that everything one perceives is an illusion? It's a preposterous idea.'

Dharma Raj: 'It seems strange, I admit. After all, what you see, hear or touch is also being experienced by everyone else similarly.'

Anirban: 'Exactly. If multiple people are sensing the same thing, then unless they are in a coordinated racket, it is an objective event and not an illusion. Human intelligence has mutated and harnessed this so-called illusory world. How can it be some kind of consensual make-believe state and not *real*?'

Gargi: 'He's right, Papa. This is when the logical mind starts rebelling. If everything is an illusion, what does *real* mean?'

Lopamudra: 'When we say that this world is not real, what we mean is that it is constantly changing. It is impermanent, limited. Physical life is maya because it does not last. Like this moment is not real because it has already become the previous moment. It is just a figment of my memory now, only as "true" as its best-kept record.'

Dharma Raj: 'And the best-kept record depends on what is perceived at that moment by our sense organs, such as they are. And this also depends on earlier recollections and memory. Our memory shapes what we perceive. Is it an example of classic self-reference? It is confusing. Which is why we need anchoring and guidance. Dare I suggest, even "parenting" by a guru. Because our sense organs can also derail us from the spiritual path.'

Nachiket: 'It isn't as if we all perceive the same thing, the same reality. Our perception is shaped by what we remember and what we expect to see. Like in the "invisible gorilla experiment".'

Lopamudra: 'What is that?'

Daniel Simons and Christopher Chabris performed an experiment in 1999 titled 'Gorillas in Our Midst: Sustained Inattentional Blindness for Dynamic Events'.[26]

Several volunteers were gathered in a basketball court. They were to observe a match. There were two teams with three players each—one team was in white shirts and the other in black. Each team passed a basketball to their teammates, either with or without dribbling. The volunteers were divided into two batches. Some were told to concentrate on the white team, others on the black team. They were also asked to count the number of passes, both with and without the dribbling. The observers did as they were told. Most of them got the count right.

During the match, a person in a full body gorilla costume walked through the staging area. On several occasions, the gorilla even thumped its chest.

The experiment was repeated several times with various batches of volunteers.

After each match, the volunteers were asked if they had noticed anything unusual—a gorilla, maybe. Almost half of them did not see the gorilla. Everyone's attention was held by the events which they were paying attention to—were *made* to pay attention to.

Thus, bias is endemic.

Gargi: 'Wow! Imagine not noticing a prancing gorilla.'

Lopamudra: '*Mayajal mein phanse the sab*!'

Anirban laughed. '*Caught in a web of illusion*! Okay!'

Lopamudra: 'Raj, I've been thinking about those three principles of *Pravrutti* you mentioned earlier. *Ekam sat vipra bahudha vadanti* is the first, right?'

Dharma Raj: 'Yes. That Truth which exists is one; the wise may speak—or know—it as many. Your truth and my truth reach the same endpoint. It's a very big idea for an individual as well as a group. It opposes the primitive, territorial mind which makes us view other people and other groups in competitive terms. Instinctively, we fight, freeze or flee when facing opposition. If we fight, one wins and the other loses. If one freezes or flees, the other wins.[27] The fight-freeze-flee instinctive response cannot accommodate any other possibility. And we carry the genetic memory of this autonomous response in our reptilian brain and hormonal system. Evolutionarily, we were animals once and that primitive brain exists within us. We may pretend we have mastered it, but it is the real master. It is the grandfather brain. It is the oldest and most powerful.'

Anirban: 'Yes, absolutely. Just like a pack of hounds protecting its territory, humans guard their psychological and ideological space. Once we secure them, we wish to expand them. It is not enough that I win an argument and leave you without a comeback. I would want to make you think the way I do.'

Nachiket: 'Yes, it makes us feel good. It makes us feel like we are better than the others. Like, "My mother is the best." "My child is the best." "My country is the best." "My ideology is the best."'

Lopamudra: '*I am the best*—who isn't convinced of that deep down? Human nature is what it will be, but when such tendencies find support in theology, they become dangerous. "My God is true; your God or Gods are false". "Other Gods, or Goddesses, must not be worshipped because my One Male God is jealous!"[28] But the Hindu approach is very different. That beautiful statement—the *Ekam sat* one—is from the Rig Veda[29], right?'

Dharma Raj: 'Yes.'

Lopamudra: 'It's a proclamation that *theologically* supports the multiplicity of paths, multiple approaches to the Truth. It's the doctrine.'

Anirban: 'Why is that so important, Aunty? Whatever may be the doctrine, human beings have an unimaginable capacity for violence. They will find some excuse or the other to fight …'

Lopamudra: 'When a religious doctrine advocates that it is the only path to God and that all other doctrines are wrong and patently evil, then we have a bigger problem on our hands. Human nature is what it is, as you rightly pointed out. Violence can and does exist deep inside us. But when religious tenets give these tendencies moral credence, then it's a lost battle. The violence then acquires a halo of a just cause.'

Dharma Raj: 'Let's keep the discussion away from politics and wars, Lopa.'

Lopamudra: 'Just saying ...'

Dharma Raj smiled and continued. 'This statement from the Rig Veda gets more interesting at the individual level. We are all uniquely different in our psychological make-up. One size does not fit all, as you often say, Lopa.'

Lopamudra: 'One doctrine, one book, one God, one way—even one set of so-called "universal values" do not hold true universally.'

Dr Adarsh: 'I see your point. People are different. What is funny to some people is crass to others. A thing that moves me to tears may appear silly to you. Children of the same parents can be totally different from birth.'

Nachiket: 'And the same person is different at different stages of their life. Sixty-year-olds are not the same person they were at twenty-five. Or even at fifty-five. They react differently to the same stimuli at different times. They are distinct and constantly changing. And so, the spiritual paths cannot be the same either.'

Anirban: 'What about community and harmony then?'

Dharma Raj: 'Harmony does not imply sameness. It cannot be achieved by becoming clones of one another or aping each other. Or even subordinating oneself to someone.'

Lopamudra: 'Look at nature if you want to understand harmony. You will notice that the possibility of harmony comes into play when two entities, whether living or non-living, interact with each other. The river flows with its own energy down the rapids or at its centre. But it's in harmony if it is gentle when it meets the banks. If not, there is disharmony.'

Anirban: 'It is up to the river then? Being gentle or not?'

Dr Adarsh laughed. 'That would be interesting to know. A river in spate causes disruption and displacement on the banks. That is disharmony.'

Anirban: 'And, the slower current in a meandering river deposits sediment on the bank. But can't a still body be harmonious?'

Dharma Raj: 'Harmony needs more than one entity. Like in music. When a combination of musical notes interacts with each other in mathematical concordance and produces a pleasing effect, there is harmony. A single note played on a piano is not harmonious. The other note needs to also be played, and the two sounds, in interaction, create harmony or disharmony. Each note is different, and a single note becomes monotonous. Two notes create a harmony when they interact well, and disharmony when they don't. But the interaction is important, for that determines the harmony and disharmony. A still body can be equanimous. Two people sitting quietly exhibit and experience harmony through an exchange of a glance. Through an exchange of energy. It is interaction.'

Nachiket: 'A picture is not harmonious if it contains only one object—say, a mountain or the sun or a tiger. There's solitary splendour, but when there are differences there is scope for harmony.'

Anirban: 'Debatable. Art theory will strongly disagree with you.'

Nachiket: 'All right, Anirban. Solitary splendour too can be harmonious. But it would then be a harmony of interacting colours and gradients, making one object.'

Lopamudra continued: 'When the point of interaction is painless and not discordant, there is harmony. If there's no friction, then each can work towards its potential and can bloom. Remember one thing—we do not interact with anyone continuously, not even the people we live with.'

Anirban: 'Growth requires friction. Friction is not a bad thing, I think.'

'You are right, Anirban,' Lopamudra smiled. 'Friction can initiate growth. So can disharmony, you know. We are not saying that friction and disharmony are bad things. Or harmony is a good thing and is the only path towards growth. When we discuss one thing, we are not automatically dismissing or negating other things. And you can call it my personal bias, but harmony has beauty. Friction does not have beauty. That's all.'

Nachiket: 'The question is: how do we make interaction harmonious and yet not lose our essence—become a white cloud? How do we avoid friction without subjugating ourselves? Or remaining superficial in our interaction?'

Dharma Raj: 'The answer lies in the next principle—twin principles, actually: *Aham brahmasmi* and *Tat tvam asi.*'

Aham brahmasmi is a *mahavakya*, or a *great sentence*, from Brihadaranyaka Upanishad. Loosely translated as *I am Brahman, I am Divine*, it explains the non-dualist stance that there is no separation between the macrocosm and the microcosm. It also suggests that how I experience myself is determined by my level of consciousness. I may experience myself as a bundle of my accumulated and current thoughts and emotions, or I may be aware of these thoughts and emotions, but experience myself as an entity that is separate from them. I may experience myself as distinct from other living forms or I may experience myself as a microcosmic component of all life.

I am everything. Everything is me.

Brihadaranyaka Upanishad comprises the last chapters of Shukla Yajurveda.[30] It is believed to have been composed around 700 BCE. It has six *adhyayas* (*parts*) and is credited to Sage Yajnavalkya. The Upanishads use the technique of dialogue to explore philosophical ideas. *Brihadaranyaka Upanishad* contains conversations between many rishis and rishikas—Yajnavalkya and his wife Maitreyi, Yajnavalkya and Gargi, Ajatashatru and Gargya, and Yajnavalkya and the philosophically inclined father of Goddess Sita, King Janak.

Tat tvam asi is a *mahavakya* from the *Chandogya Upanishad*. It translates as *You are That. You are Divine. You are Everything*. The *jivatma*, or *individual soul*, is the same as *Paramatma*, or *Supreme Soul*, in its pure state. This great sentence appears at the end of each section of the *Chandogya Upanishad*.

The *Chandogya Upanishad* comprises the last chapters of Sama Veda and is believed to have been written around 800 BCE. It is credited to Sage Uddaalaka and large parts of it are set up as a conversation between the sage and his son, Shvetaketu.

Shvetaketu returns home from the *gurukul* after finishing his formal education. However, upon questioning his proud son, Uddaalaka realizes that Shvetaketu has

returned only with a theoretical understanding of life and
the nature of reality. His gurukul has failed to translate
knowledge into a lived experience or realization. Thus
starts the conversation, with the remark, 'You are That,
Shvetaketu!'[31]

Dr Adarsh: 'My *dadamoshay* (*grandfather*), often said,
"I am everything; I am everywhere." Egotistical thought,
don't you think? Very arrogant, and with no humility.
I hate to admit it, but a bit like him. He was very
inconsiderate of everyone around him and had an inflated
sense of self. The family suffered. *Aham Brahmasmi* ...
My *dadamoshay* was everything!'

Lopamudra: '*Dadamoshay*! You remind me how sweet
our Bengali tongue is. Yes, ideas can be misleading unless
properly understood. "I am everything". Who is this "I"?
Understanding that is the challenge.'

Anirban: '*Nijam*.'

Gargi: 'What's *nijam*?'

Anirban: '*True* in Telugu. I thought I'd throw in
a bit of my mother tongue as well! Anyway, yes, the
ego pursues gratification, secure in the belief that it is
supreme. *Aham Brahmasmi!*'

Nachiket: 'Papa, you had said this to me once—that
our mistaken identity is not divine. "Nachiket" is not

the divine permanent. "Nachiket" is my temporary identity. The eternal "I" that dwells within us is the divine permanent.'

Dharma Raj: 'It's very difficult to get around our swollen ego. But the *Chandogya Upanishad* offers a balancing idea, a "yin" to the "yang" of *Aham brahmasmi*. That "yin" is *Tat tvam asi. Your essence, too, is divine. Everything is part of the same element that makes you.*'

Lopamudra: 'I am the centre. You are the centre. The centre is everywhere.'

Anirban: 'I remember hearing that recently in another context. Oh, yes, that old Sioux story.'

Dr Adarsh: 'What story?'

Black Elk was a Sioux boy born to the Oglala Lakota family that lived along the Little Powder River in South Dakota in the second half of the nineteenth century.

The boy fell ill at age nine. Days passed, and he showed no signs of improvement. The worried parents called the local shaman. As the shaman examined the boy, Black Elk trembled and began to have a Great Vision. He later reported that he saw himself 'on the central mountain of the world, the highest place'.

To the child, the central mountain was the Harney Peak. It has since been renamed the Black Elk Peak.

His words expanded the very definition of 'centre'. He said, '*The central mountain is everywhere* ... Anywhere is the centre of the world.'[32]

The Sioux are a Native American tribe that lived around the source of the Mississippi river. Their habitat spread across modern-day Nebraska, Montana, Minnesota, and North and South Dakota.

Anirban: 'Joseph Campbell says that seeing yourself as the centre can be "raw individualism" unless you understand that the centre is also in front of you, in the person you face. That person, too, is your centre.'[33]

Dharma Raj: 'Exactly. *That* is the secret of harmony. Respectful inclusion.'

'How do I generate it within me? How do I generate it in the people around me? Easier said than done,' Dr Adarsh said uneasily.

Anirban glanced at his friend discreetly. He knew that Adarsh and his wife, Mona, were going through a rough patch in their marriage.

Dharma Raj: 'I would say, look to Nature for answers. Nature teaches us when it is in balance and when it is in imbalance. Let us focus on the harmony and balance aspect first. The river nourishes the tree, and the tree provides food. It also becomes home for the birds.

Bird droppings feed the earthworm, and the earthworm improves soil health ... There is a connection among them all, and their respectful interaction allows life to flourish.'

Lopamudra: 'And they also preserve their uniqueness. So, harmony and respect are intertwined. When nature is in a state of respectful inclusion, there is harmony. When it isn't, there is disharmony.'

Dr Adarsh: 'The disharmony is not very respectful, is it? There's violence in nature, killing and getting killed. The prey and the predator interaction ... would you call it disrespectful?'

Dharma Raj: 'The prey–predator relationship is nature's ordained way but there's no reason to believe that they do not respect each other. Taking each other seriously is respectful, I would think. The predator hunts, the prey gets hunted. This is the nature of their interaction. They're not friends. They *cannot* be friends. But there's plenty of respect in that interaction. It is natural predatory behaviour, the smooth functioning of which retains balance in life. Do you remember the lion and doe story from Amish's book *Raavan: Enemy of Aryavarta*?'

Gargi: 'Yes, I do ... one of my favourite scenes! There is magnificence in both the hunter and the hunted, depending on why they do what they do. When we take each other seriously, there is respect. Disrespect is careless and dismissive.'

Anirban: 'And in the animal world, it can be dangerous. If you're careless, you are dead. But aren't these human notions? Respect? Friendship? And where is the evidence that there is any relationship between prey and predator besides them looking at each other as "food" and "danger"?'

Gargi: 'Metaphor and extrapolation too are human notions, right, Anirban? And what about building narratives to convey ideas? For example, in *The Lion King*[34], Timon and Pumbaa are Simba's "friends". Mufasa explains the concept of respect to Simba. He also demonstrates it. Using animal behaviour to explain human notions is a very old technique. Reason and logic are merely one aspect of human intelligence. *Theek hai?* (*Okay?*)'

Dr Adarsh: 'Wow! Do you two always fight like this? I don't understand how you are friends!'

Gargi: 'Oh! We are great friends! Sometimes with, sometimes without respect!! Right, Anirban?'

Anirban ducked, avoiding a mock blow. And laughed. 'You're the craziest friend I have, Gargi Sawant.'

Dharma Raj raised his eyebrows with a hint of a smile on his face. Nachiket looked at his wife with sheer delight.

Anirban: 'There's one more thing. It may be unrelated, but I need to say this. Violence is a very small part of animal interactions. I'm a photographer and I'm telling you, TV shows do not represent the complete picture. They showcase the kills majorly—I suppose because viewers like watching that stuff. But most of the time animals in a jungle are peaceful. Prey and predator exist in close proximity, in peace. The predator is not hungry all the time and only kills when hungry.'

Dr Adarsh: 'The larger point you are making is that harmony can exist even if there's an element of violence. Is that so?'

Lopamudra: 'That's a thought worth examining.'

Dharma Raj: 'I don't know the answer. One thing we know is that human beings don't live in harmony, either with nature or with one another. We are destroying nature for our needs and for some unattainable satisfaction. But we are only trying to fill a bottomless pit.'

Nachiket: 'What can satisfy us then?'

Dr Adarsh laughed. 'No clue. But we could begin with giving respect. We could try to respect each other while interacting.'

Nachiket: 'Disrespect leads to disharmony, and we see a lot of it today. We give it a variety of names—religious conflict, misunderstanding, angst, vengeance, prejudice, intolerance, moral arrogance, activism and doing good. But all this happens because we lack respect.'

Dr Adarsh: 'People even fight for their right to offend. To make fun of others ... all for the right to be disrespectful.'

Gargi: '*Hona chahiye na*? (*Should it not be so?*) We need these rights.'

Lopamudra: 'I suppose so. They serve as pressure valves. If we use friction appropriately, it can be useful. But remember that it will also cause disharmony. Disrespect creates disharmony, but suppressing the right to say whatever we want is worse.'

Dharma Raj: 'Someday, our species will learn to disagree without being disrespectful. Till then, the exercise of freedom without respect is likely to cause disharmony. Accept that.'

Anirban: 'Hmm. What is the third principle?'

Dharma Raj: '*Ishaavasyam idam sarvam*; *Yatkincha jagatyaam jagat*. Gargi, there's a beautiful translation of the *Isha Upanishad* lying on my desk. It's by Pritish Nandy. Can you get it for me? I want to read out some bits I like.'

Gargi got up and went into her parents' room. Just then, the doorbell rang and there was the sound of the gate creaking open. Nachiket stepped out to take the food packets from the delivery boy and went into the kitchen with them. The others sat back, suddenly conscious of their growling stomachs.

9

TO BE, IS TO BE DIVINE

Dr Adarsh's phone was ringing incessantly and he finally moved away from the group to answer it. He walked back in, looking relieved.

'All good?' Anirban asked him cautiously.

Dr Adarsh: 'Yep! It was Mona. She said if I'm enjoying this evening so much, I can relax on one condition—repeat the conversation to her tomorrow. Verbatim.'

Dharma Raj: 'Why don't you ask her to join us?'

Dr Adarsh: 'I did ask, but she laughed and said she has no interest in such conversations. The *mayavi* world is very real to her.'

Lopamudra: 'Or it could be her way of giving you space. That's sweet.'

Dr Adarsh: 'Really? Hmmm ... I didn't look at it that way.'

Nachiket and Gargi returned, the former carrying a tray and the latter holding the book.

'Here's some kande pohe, idlis and samosas. Gargi, can you please fetch the tray from the dining table? I've poured the coffee already.'

Gargi: 'Sure. And here's the book for you, Papa.'

Dharma Raj took the book from her and leafed through it till he found the right page. The rest helped themselves to the delicious food. Lopamudra filled a plate with kande pohe and placed it on the coffee table next to her husband. Gargi came back with a trayful of coffee cups.

Dharma Raj: 'Here it is:

Ishaavasyam idam sarvam; Yatkincha jagatyaam jagat.
He exists in all that lives.
Renounce all which pass away.
Rejoice in that which lives forever.[35]

It is the first verse of the *Isha Upanishad*. The overriding message is that God pervades everything. Everything is divine.'

Isha Upanishad is one of the ten principal Upanishads. It is a small Upanishad written at the end of the Shukla Yajurveda. It has only eighteen mantras, but they have served as a driving force for philosophers of the calibre of Adi Shankaracharya, Swami Chinmayananda, Sri Aurobindo, Mahatma Gandhi and Vinoba Bhave. It presents Vedantic thought in a nutshell.

Mahatma Gandhi said of this Upanishad, 'If all the Upanishads and all the other scriptures happened all of a sudden to be reduced to ashes, and if only the first verse in the *Ishopanishad* were left in the memory of the Hindus, Hinduism would live forever.'

Nachiket: 'Basically, if it exists, it is Godly—the trees, the rivers, the mountains, the forests …'

Dr Adarsh: 'The animals, the birds, the bees …'

Gargi: 'The stars, the planets, the Sun, the Moon …'

Lopamudra: 'The man, the woman, the sticks and stones …'

Anirban: 'Especially the stones fashioned into idols?'

Lopamudra: 'Remember that old song from the movie *Kalicharan*? *"Patthar ki puja karke, haari main haari"*?'

Gargi: 'I have a different take on the song. *Patthar ki puja karke, na haari main na haari!* How would you translate *my* version, Nachiket?'

Nachiket: '"*Worshipping stones as I have, I've not lost, no I've not lost!*" Doesn't quite carry the same punch when translated.'

Anirban: 'Aunty, it is interesting that you bunched man and woman with sticks and stones. Was that intentional, your linking man and woman to sticks and stones?'

Lopamudra smiled. 'No, it wasn't consciously intentional.'

Dr Adarsh: 'I like that—consciously intentional. Real intentions often sit in our unconscious'

Anirban: 'It appeared like a force fit to me, but I think it was deliberate on your part.'

He wiggled his eyebrows mischievously, and continued, 'You are trying to remove our in-built feeling of separateness from other forms of life, I think. Also, most of us would classify sticks as a life form—plant life—but stones? And then I remembered reading an article by Robert Hazen, a mineralogist. He said that there has been a systemic increase in the number of species of rocks and their complexity over time. Minerals exhibit evolution. And they are evolving rapidly today due to human activities.'[36]

Nachiket: 'The Anthropocene era. We human beings are dramatically affecting the pace of evolution on this planet.'

Gargi: 'And, thus, rock is life! If it evolves then it is life.'

Lopamudra: 'I suppose I wish to question the separateness that we humans experience from other forms of life. The human point of view has to come in because we are human. But our observation of nature and life must include us. We are not outside of it.'

Nachiket: 'Okay, so, everything is divine. Fine. But to what purpose? What's the ultimate purpose of life?'

Dharma Raj: 'Ultimate purpose ... well, the entire universe is in an endless cycle of repetition. Rhythmic repetition. But there's also a yearning to reach a state of balance. It never attains this balance, but the pursuit is always on, non-stop. So, the purpose is balance, I think.'

Lopamudra: 'And we forget too often that we too are a part of the universe. So, in some sense, our inner spirit yearns for balance as well. We try to ignore the need, but it persists.'

Anirban: 'Confucius said that harmony within society is possible only when there is internal harmony, that is, harmony within each person in that society. According to him internal harmony leads to harmony in the family, the state, the world, and ultimately the universe.'[37]

Dr Adarsh: 'What is internal harmony anyway? A person can appear calm and completely at peace, and yet be angry or troubled inside.'

Dharma Raj: 'That's it. That would be disharmony. Harmony is not about appearance. There is internal harmony when our innermost thoughts do not differ from our words, our deepest emotions are not at odds with our actions. And our actions do not contradict our words, thoughts and emotions.'

Dr Adarsh: 'That's not always possible. Do you know anyone like that?'

Dharma Raj: 'No—we are human after all. But it should be possible someday. Some time. In some life. At some future point. We can work towards it.'

Anirban: 'Through idol worship?!'

Anirban looked at Dharma Raj incredulously, but the man remained calm and held his gaze steadily. Lopamudra couldn't stand the disrespect being shown to Dharma Raj, and rebuked Anirban's discomfort-laced curiosity about the subject. Trying her best not to raise her voice, she said, 'Don't practise idol worship, Anirban, if you don't want to. But don't scoff at it. Because that is the first step towards extremism, the first step towards hating someone just because they practise idol worship.'

Anirban: 'I'm sorry, that was rude. I'm really sorry, Aunty. But I am not able to relate to idol worship or even understand it. God knows I have tried. For my mother's sake.'

Dharma Raj: 'Patience, Anirban. We're talking about internal harmony right now.'

Nachiket: 'And how do we attain internal harmony?'

Dharma Raj: 'By first understanding our temperament—*really* understanding it. It is critical that we do that. Actually, this is connected to what modern psychology calls our "unconscious". It is not easy to understand it because we are not aware of many aspects of ourselves. Our temperament is connected to our unconscious and is sometimes clearer to others than to us.'

Gargi: 'We may not know some part of ourselves, I agree. Yes, there is the unconscious, but surely we have a pretty good idea of who we are? Or do you think we are all psychos? Just plain delusional about ourselves?'

Dharma Raj: 'There you go, Gargi, the blithe spirit without filters. Incidentally, you're thinking in extremes again. Why choose immoderate words? You'll lose the listener like this.'

Gargi pursed her lips. 'Okay, then we are all Alices and Toms in Wonderland. We don't know who we are.'

Dharma Raj sighed deeply. He glanced at Nachiket and saw him looking at Gargi with an amused expression.

Dharma Raj always noticed his son-in-law's unease with her non-empathic ways and unfiltered behaviour, and it made him defensive about his daughter. He pursed his lips as his protectiveness towards her rose to the surface. His disapproval quickly shifted from daughter to son-in-law. Human weaknesses are deep and unfathomable, after all.

Dr Adarsh: 'I see that. We *think* we know ourselves, but we don't. We cocoon ourselves in rationalizations and psychological comfort.'

Dharma Raj: 'We may not completely know ourselves, but we do know what we like to think about ourselves. In any case, what we consciously know about ourselves is the tip of the iceberg. The rest is unknown. We do not know the part of our nature that was well-formed by the time we were two years old, for instance. According to studies, a good part of our basic nature is formed during cell formation in the womb.'[38]

Dr Adarsh: 'It is called cell memory.'

Dharma Raj: 'Yes, it's very powerful. Our temperament is largely developed before we learn our first word. It happens through maternal imprinting and mirroring, mostly. Even as infants, our sense organs perceive and our brain records, and our emotions are prompted by what we record, unconsciously. Once we learn words and begin to speak, our understanding is shaped by words, but our emotional base is already laid out. So, it's not a part of our conscious self-understanding.'

Gargi: 'How is it created? Biologically, I mean.'

Dr Adarsh: 'Through chemical tags on our genes, for one. Epigenetics. Events, emotions, what we perceive— they become a part of our DNA. Siddhartha Mukherjee puts it very poetically in his book *The Gene*.[39] He says the smell of the madeleine you enjoyed in Paris made a chemical tag on your gene—*epigenetic marks are gradually layered above genes*. That smell will arouse the same emotions every single time. And epigenetic alterations are inherited. So, the smell of the madeleine may have been your grandmom's experience. You will love it too, even if you have never been to Paris!'

Dharma Raj: 'We must discuss this further someday, probably when we talk about the chakras. For now, what we can say is that it's tough to uncover our *svabhava* (*temperament*). Perhaps we do not need to at all, in an intellectual sense. It only needs to be overwritten by building our *charitra* (*character*).'

Dr Adarsh: 'How?'

Lopamudra: 'With *buddhi* and *vivek*. (*Intellect* and *wisdom/discernment*.) Like Papa said, the how-to would have to be another discussion, but we must first recognize our temperament. And self-understanding leads to internal transformation. Our *Ishta Devatas* can help us with this. But first, we need the blessings of a Greek God. Have you heard of God Kairos?'

Anirban: 'The Greek God of the Right Moment!'

Lopamudra smiled.

God Chronos/Cronus, the Titan God of Time and Space, is married to Goddess Rhea, mother of the Olympian Gods.[40] But Chronos does not wish to have children. He is afraid that history will repeat itself and they will overthrow Him, just as He had once overthrown His father, Uranus. So, whenever Rhea gives birth, Chronos swallows the child immediately. Feeling helpless, Rhea finally gives birth to Zeus and takes control of Her child's destiny. When Chronos approaches Her to take the new-born away, She hands over a rock wrapped in a cloth to Her husband. Chronos immediately swallows the piece of rock, imagining it is His new-born child. Rhea then hides Zeus on the island of Crete where Her son is nursed by Amaltheia the goat.

One day, Zeus learns about His father and returns. He tears open the stomach of Chronos and releases His brothers and sisters: Poseidon, the God of the

Seas; Hades, the God of the Underworld; Demeter, the Goddess of Agriculture; Hestia, the Goddess of the Hearth; and Hera, the Goddess of Marriage and Family.

Zeus, the God of Thunder and Lightning, marries Hera and becomes the king of the Gods and Goddesses, presiding over Mount Olympus, the home of the Gods. He has many children with Hera: Ares, the God of War; Hephaestus, the God of Fire; and Hebe, the Goddess of Youth. He also has children from other women: the Gods Apollo, Hermes and Dionysus and the Goddesses Artemis and Athena (His favourite child).

His youngest child is God Kairos. If Chronos is the God of Sequential Time, then Kairos, His grandchild, is the God of Breakthrough Time—the right moment.[41]

Kairos is young and good-looking, with a single lock of hair that falls dramatically over His forehead. The back of His head is bald and smooth, suggesting that He is 'un-grabbable' from behind—you can only seize Him from the front. He has wings on His feet as well as His back, implying that He is fleet-footed. Often, He's depicted as standing on tiptoe: now you see Him, now you don't. The opportune moment stands on a knife-edge, and so He holds a knife in one hand.

Kairos and Tyche, the Goddess of Fortune and Luck, are lovers. They belong together, because they create a 'magical moment'—union of the right moment and good fortune.

The Ancient Greek poet Posidippus wrote some evocative lines on this elusive God, represented in a statue sculpted by the classical sculptor, Lysippos:

'Who and from where is the sculptor? From Sicyon. And his name? Lysippos.

And who are you? Kairos, the all subduer.

Why do you stand on tiptoe? I am always running.

Why do you have a pair of wings on your feet? I fly with the wind.

Why do you hold a razor in your right hand? As a sign to men that I am sharper than any sharp edge.

And why is your hair over your face? For the one who meets me to grasp at, by Zeus.

And why is the back of your head bald? Because none whom I have once raced by on my winged feet will now, though he wishes it, take hold of me from behind.

Why did the artist fashion you? For your sake, stranger, and he set me up in the portico as a lesson.'[42]

Nachiket: 'Wow! That's neat. The God of the Right Moment. What does he do?'

Lopamudra: 'He's the God of that mystic moment in communication when the speaker's words are received by the listener without distortion or misunderstanding.'

Gargi: 'Is that really so rare as to merit a God? Miscommunication occurs occasionally, I agree, but everyone talks all the time. And messages still get across.'

Dharma Raj: 'It is rare. Very, very rare, and you know that. Of course, the speaker must choose the right words to communicate what he or she wants to say, which is a challenge, especially when emotions are involved. Emotions can ambush conversations. But, more importantly, the listener must listen to the words honestly, unfiltered by their own biases and prejudices and implicit agenda, which is almost impossible. No wonder the Greeks put a God in charge of it.'

Gargi: 'Communicating with whom exactly?'

Dharma Raj: 'Anybody, everybody. Especially with those who are closest to us. But the most important communication is the one inside our head. We delude ourselves all the time. Our self-talk is often an agenda-led conversation with ourselves, without us being conscious of our underlying motives. We want to feel good about ourselves, come what may. And this is where idolatry can play a subtle role.'

Lopamudra: 'Self-understanding doesn't come easily. We need guidance, or at least signposts of some sort. And that's how the Gods can help us. And for this, they must be *saguna* (*possessing qualities*).'

Nachiket: 'Unlike the *Nivruttic* path where "Godhood" would be *nirguna* (*without qualities*). Right?'

Dharma Raj: 'And *niraakar* (*without form*). Each God or Goddess has distinct qualities, just like we possess different qualities. We need that resonance, that harmonic motion.'

Anirban: 'Interesting that you say "harmonic motion". That's a concept in physics.'

Lopamudra: 'Yes, but here the concept is applied to the emotional body. My quality then becomes louder, clearer, as a result of reinforcement from the reflected vibration.'

Gargi: 'Ma, can you explain that? I did not follow it.'

Lopamudra: 'Gargi, when soldiers cross a suspension bridge, they break step. They do not march in unison over the bridge. Do you know why?'

Gargi: 'No. I don't.'

Lopamudra: 'Because, when soldiers march in step, they generate one common frequency. And if that frequency matches the frequency of the suspended bridge, then the mechanical resonance amplifies the natural vibration of the bridge greatly, and it comes apart.'

Gargi: 'Aah. And you are applying this concept to emotions. When my emotions resonate with the symbolic resonance of a deity, they get amplified and rise to the surface. They become recognizable.'

Nachiket: 'Therefore, different *Ishta Devatas* for different people.'

Lopamudra: 'Sorry, Raj, but I can't help making a small political point here.'

Dharma Raj smiled. 'If you insist. You do have a penchant for it.'

Lopamudra smiled back. 'Thank you. Life is diverse, we all know that. And we must *experience* that real inclusive unity and love towards everything and everyone that religious and even moralistic people love to talk about. Practising inclusion with a large heart is different than with the mind. Without involving the heart, if we are told that there is only one God, then that God becomes mine and my people's. We set ourselves up for intolerance and disharmony with this selective inclusion. If "I" or "my people" are right, then "you" or the "others" must be wrong. This is inevitable.'

Anirban: 'How do you come to this conclusion? Intolerance and disharmony will happen regardless of any "experienced understanding". Aren't you generalizing too much?'

Lopamudra: 'Anirban, I'm making a distinction between understanding with the mind, through thought, and understanding with the heart, through experience and feeling it. A truly kind heart *cannot* be intolerant and disharmonious towards anyone. And I'm not talking about kindness towards one person or some people. I'm talking about a heart that *feels* kindness. Always.'

Anirban: 'So, this intolerance would happen even if the message of love and fraternity was delivered by a prophet who experienced oneness with everyone and everything? Who *felt* no otherness?'

Lopamudra: 'Yes, I would assume so. Unity and respectful inclusion are the *prophet's* experience, not that of his followers. *He* felt them, not his followers—not even many of his first followers. For them "one God" is a *belief*. They *think* it. And they receive the message in the form of exclusivity or separateness. Selective inclusion. It makes them special, the "chosen ones". The message of unity and respect for all is almost completely lost at the first point of exchange.'

Gargi: '*He* is their experience. His experience is not their experience. It is their belief.'

Nachiket: 'Communication is not a simple process. Often, we talk at cross-purposes, don't we, Gargi?'

Gargi: 'You twist what I say.'

Nachiket: 'I don't do it deliberately, I assure you.'

Gargi: 'Okay then, I admit I am sometimes unable to say things the way I want to with you. Emotions get in the way, right? I must spend more time trying to understand myself and then gain mastery over my emotions.'

Nachiket: 'So must I.'

Gargi: 'Not too much, though. It will take away all the fun!'

Nachiket smiled.

Dr Adarsh: 'So, God is an experience, not a belief. Self-understanding too is an experience and not a belief. A feeling and not just thoughts.'

Nachiket: 'Gods, Adarsh. I agree. Experiencing something, and thinking or believing it, are different things sometimes. When we think about something, we can either understand it or be unsure about what we are thinking. We either reach a conclusion, or not. But when we feel something, there is no scope for uncertainty. We know ...'

Gargi: 'It's like falling in love.[43] You think you understand what it is. But you fall in love and then you know you did not understand it at all. The madness. All the Mills & Boon nonsense of your teenage years evaporates in the air.'

Anirban raised his eyebrows.

Gargi: 'Yes, Anirban, Mills & Boon books are superficial and don't teach anything about love. But I completely enjoyed them in my teenage years. Also, Barbara Cartland and Norma Klien. Go ahead, you can laugh.'

Anirban: 'Sorry. I didn't mean to judge.'

Nachiket: 'Of course, our thoughts can make us deny what we are feeling. *Jaan ke anjaan*. The mind is powerful. Yet, if you open up to what you are feeling, you are sure. You know, without a doubt then, that you are feeling angry, or are afraid ... Anyway, tell us about the *Ishta Devatas* and the possibility of experiencing our qualities, Papa, Ma.'

Dharma Raj: 'It's simple, actually. Just as your body needs props to exercise, so also does *aatmagyaan* (*self-knowledge*). It needs a lot of props—customized props. The goal is inner integration. There should be no contradiction in your emotions, self-talk, talking to others and behaviour.'

Lopamudra: 'Both symbols and mythology serve as subtle, indirect props. They're hooks.'

Dr Adarsh: 'In science, symbols and diagrams are used as images which represent complex ideas. So, do idols represent a certain philosophy of life and ideas?'

Lopamudra: 'Idols can *also* represent ideas. Right now, that is what we are suggesting. They can be personifications of our tendencies, impulses and traits. They've gathered collective energy over millennia. Their messages have been relayed down the ages.'

Anirban: 'The Swiss psychiatrist Carl Jung was greatly influenced by our Gods and Goddesses. He called them archetypes embedded in our collective unconscious.'

Dharma Raj: 'That's what symbols are. Something material that represents something non-material. They simply represent something else.'

Anirban: 'Rather a simple definition. What is this "something else"?'

Gargi: '"Telling someone what a symbol 'meant' was like telling them how a song should make them feel—it was different for all people."[44] I remember reading that in a Robert Langdon novel. The line stayed with me.'

Dr Adarsh: 'Who is Robert Langdon?'

Anirban: 'He's a fictional character. Don't tell me you haven't heard of *The Da Vinci Code*, Adarsh.'

Dr Adarsh: 'I've watched the movie.'

Gargi: 'The book is much better.'

Anirban: 'Books are always better than movies, aren't they?'

Gargi: 'Not necessarily. *Gone with the Wind*. *Chariots of Fire*. Our very own *Guide*.'[45]

Anirban: 'I've always preferred the books.'

Gargi: '*Bourne Identity*?'[46]

Anirban: 'You've got me there. The movie is definitely better.'

Nachiket: 'Talking about movies and books always makes me hungry for some reason. Shall I call in for some pizzas for dinner? Papa?'

'Extra cheese for me, please,' Dharma Raj winked.

Nachiket: 'I don't think so! Thin crust with a healthy topping of vegetables, that's what we should all get. You've just returned from the hospital!'

Dharma Raj: 'I'm all right now. *Marna ek hi baar hai!*'

Everyone laughed.

Gargi: 'We only die once … Meanwhile, can I get some wine, Papa?'

Dharma Raj: 'Of course.'

Lopamudra: 'Gargi, there are some bottles in the refrigerator. Papa picked up some superb Sangiovese from the mall last week.'

Anirban: 'Italian?'

Dharma Raj: 'No, Indian wine from Fratelli. Frankly, I was amazed at the quality. Indian winemaking has come a long way.'

Lopamudra: 'Papa also picked up a fancy wine aerator. So, you don't have to decant the wine and wait. It's in the top drawer in the kitchen, along with the knives and forks.'

Gargi: 'Wow, you guys are becoming wine connoisseurs! Let's try some.'

10

LOVE, SOLACE AND HOPE

Gargi Sawant was a connoisseur of small pleasures. She enjoyed red and white wines equally and loved to experiment. She poured out the wine for everyone.

Dr Adarsh: 'Not for me, Gargi.'

Gargi: 'Why not?'

Dr Adarsh: 'I'm a doctor. Always on call. Also, I'm given to extremes. Better to be safe than sorry.'

Gargi sat, swirled the wine around in her glass, sniffed and took a small sip. 'Mmmm ... Nice. I never knew we made such good wines. Only Indian wines for me from now on.'

Anirban: 'Famous last words!'

Nachiket smiled.

Lopamudra: 'There are many excellent wineries in India. You have a wide range to choose from.'

Anirban: 'You know, it is believed that Dionysus—'

Nachiket: 'The Greek God of Wine.'

Anirban: 'Also the Greek God of Enthusiasm. An ancient Greek legend holds that Dionysus brought wine to India from Greece.'[47]

Dharma Raj: 'Interesting. I like this God of Enthusiasm. My kind of God!'

Dr Adarsh: 'When you're enthusiastic, you're joyful, and when you're joyful, you experience the divine.'

Zeus, the God of Thunder and Lightning, was also known as the God of the Sky.[48] Although He lived on Mount Olympus, He was known to visit humans and interact with them. One day He fell in love with Semele, a human. Dionysus was born of this union, but Semele tragically died.

Dionysus is chiefly known as the Greek God of Wine. He is also the God of Exuberance, Theatre, Nature, Enthusiasm and, even, Madness. In some sense, He's the God of Chaos, philosophically contrasted with another son of Zeus, Apollo, who is the God of Order. Unhinged exuberance can lead to religious ecstasy sometimes, and therein lies the magical possibility of Dionysus. If you avoid the pitfalls, that is. The psychology of theatre and drama embody the psychology of life, and life can ensnare you into unbalance.

Midas, king of Lydia, pleased Dionysus with his kindness.[49] As a gesture of goodwill, Dionysus granted Midas a boon. The foolish king asked that whatever he touches should turn to gold. Dionysus acceded. Alas, this Dionysian boon eventually drove poor Midas to madness. His food turned to gold, his drink turned to gold, the roses in his garden turned to gold and even his daughter turned to gold when he reached out to comfort her. We call this ironic affliction the Midas Touch.

Gargi: 'Sometimes *bhakti* generates Dionysian joy and exuberance.'

Lopamudra: 'Yes. *Bhakti* is a good place to start our discussion on the Hindu Gods and Goddesses. It draws out sweet sentiments in us and it can arrest the wanderings of our mind. It makes us feel love that goes beyond "me" and "my own". Most of us are deeply interested only in "my own". Those who are outside this circle interest us only if they impact us. Devotional love can expand us. It is a peculiar longing and can fill our hearts with ecstasy. It can make us rise above our limitations and sometimes even release our ego.'

Dharma Raj: 'At least in theory. Often, *bhakti* is connected to our fears and desires and is trapped by the ego.'

Nachiket: 'So *bhakti* can become dangerous too, then. You start hating the "other", who does not align with the object of your own *bhakti*, be it your God or your country. Take for example, I am a bhakt of my country. I could choose to become a soldier, a sculptor creating a statue for a street corner or a scientist sending Mangalyaan to Mars. I could be a police officer protecting my society, a law enforcer like Papa. Or I could just spend my time hating other countries and people and venting.'

Gargi: 'Social media is often used as a platform for venting.'

Dr Adarsh: 'Not fair. Social media platforms help me unwind. But let us get back on track. What makes for a good bhakt?'

Lopamudra smiled: 'There's no good or bad bhakt. *Bhakti* just brings underlying feelings to the surface; it can actually show you who you are. It can also be an inner movement toward self-understanding.'

Anirban: 'There is a possibility that it may not happen.'

Lopamudra: 'Maybe not. But that's all right. There's always the next life for us Hindus!'

Anirban: 'We Hindus mention the prospect of the next life with casual ease, don't we?'

Nachiket: 'The concept of the next life subliminally takes away the urgency and pressure of reaching realization. It also brings inertia, I suppose. Anyway, a devotional heart is enough for experiencing a fraternal connection. Like, singing kirtans in a group can be thrilling. It always makes me feel good.'

Lopamudra: '*Bhakti* also gives solace and hope ... hope remained in Pandora's box, didn't it, Anirban?'

Prometheus, one of the Titans, incurs the wrath of God Zeus, king of the Gods, when he steals fire from the Gods and gifts it to the mortals.[50] Zeus metes out a terrible punishment for this affront. He binds Prometheus to a stake on Mount Caucasus and He tasks an eagle to pick at his liver every morning. The liver regrows during the night, only for the torture to commence all over again in the morning. Prometheus writhes on Mount Caucasus, waiting to be unbound.

Mankind too is punished for having accepted the gift of fire. Zeus asks Hephaestus, the divine craftsman, to forge a woman from clay. He names her Pandora and bestows upon her a jar full of 'gifts'. Curiously, He also tells her to never open the jar—it must remain shut, always. Zeus sends Pandora to Epimetheus, brother of Prometheus, who accepts her as his wife despite Prometheus having warned him to not accept gifts from Zeus. In Greek mythology, Prometheus signifies 'forethought', while Epimetheus signifies 'afterthought'.

Epimetheus and Pandora are unable to contain their curiosity and open the jar. Miseries, diseases and evils billow out and spread on Earth. Pandora quickly snaps the jar shut and wails with a terrible foreboding. But then a faint sound wafts into her ears—a faint tinkle. Her eyes detect a glimmer emanating from the jar. Hope had remained nestled within. It had not escaped.

Never despair, for Hope never leaves.

Anirban: 'So it did! Hope did not escape.'

Lopamudra: 'Hmmm. Solace and hope are not easy to find, but self-understanding—it is a lot of hard work. Symbols and myths help because the approach is indirect and non-threatening. Non-confrontational. They are correlative—images and stories evoke intuition and emotions.'

Nachiket: 'So, it's not about the intellect or knowledge. They can be like clues.'

Anirban: 'And it's certainly not literal. I like that.'

Dharma Raj: 'It *cannot* be literal or direct, because the ego then owns the direct message and it quickly becomes about others and takes us away from self-reflection.'

Nachiket: 'How do we recognize the ego?'

Anirban: 'Joseph Campbell said something interesting. He said the ego cannot reflect upon itself. So, it needs a mirror to map itself.'[51]

Dharma Raj: 'And the Gods can serve as mirrors. Yes, I like that, Anirban.'

Anirban: 'The question is, what do we want to see in the mirror?'

Lopamudra: 'Begin with not *wanting* to see.'

Dharma Raj: 'Which brings us back to Ma's *Ishta Devata*. You do not choose your *Ishta Devata*. Your *Ishta Devata* chooses you, depending on your *samskaras* or tendencies.'

Gargi: 'Temperament, right?'

Lopamudra slowly shook her head. 'Yeeesss, sort of. *Samskaras* are psychological impressions, even some inclinations. We are born with our *samskara*—it's *our spontaneous expression*. It's innate. *Temperament—svabhava*—is also a product of social conditioning which enhances or encumbers it. *Samskara* and *svabhava* ... not personality so much as its tendency.'

Dr Adarsh: 'It becomes evident from the first few months of life. I have a twin, you know—Shirish.'

Nachiket: 'Really? I didn't know that.'

Dr Adarsh smiled fondly. 'I don't talk about him much. We may be twins, but we're like chalk and cheese. I was sickly, even at birth; he was robust. Within six months, kakas and mamis were gravitating towards him ... As a toddler he was cheerful and courageous, hot-tempered, unafraid and impulsive. I was quiet and risk-averse, cautious and grumpy. He was unkempt; I was fastidious. He was flamboyant; I was restrained.'

Lopamudra: 'Temperament and tendencies are inherent. Character building requires effort and is a responsibility.'

Dharma Raj: 'We can choose not to exercise this responsibility. But then, our innate temperament slowly takes over. And worsens. It's not easy to change, or even truly recognize our temperament.'

Lopamudra: 'Lord Ganesh can help us. He moderates our temperament and gives us the tools for character development—once we make the choice.'

Goddess Parvati decides to have a leisurely bath while Lord Shiva is away.[52] Not wanting to be disturbed, She fashions a child from *chandan* (*sandalwood*) paste and breathes life into it. She then commands Her son to stand guard outside the bath and not allow entry to anyone.

Meanwhile, Lord Shiva returns home and wants to see His wife. But the child will not let Him in. Enraged, the Lord chops off the head of the resolute guard. However, on learning the truth of the loyal doorman's identity from His distraught wife, Lord Shiva directs the faithful Nandi to set forth and bring back the head of the first creature he encounters. Nandi returns with the head of an elephant, which Lord Shiva promptly attaches to the child's body. The large-hearted Lord Nataraj instantly accepts Lord Ganesh, the little one, as His own.

Lord Ganesh, the son of Lord Shiva and Goddess Parvati, is also the brother of Lord Kartikeya, the commander of the army of the Gods. In North India, Lord Ganesh is the younger brother while in South India He is elder. He is the husband of Riddhi and Siddhi, who represent prosperity and wisdom, and the father of

Shubha and Labha, who represent auspiciousness and gain.

He has many names—Ganpati, Vinayaka, Prathamesha, Vakratunda, Ekadanta, Lambodara, Gajananda, Pillaiyar and so on.

He has an elephant head and a potbelly. His upper left hand holds the *pasha* (*lasso*). In His lower left hand, He holds a laddoo or modak. His upper right hand holds a *parashu* (*axe*). And He holds His lower right hand up, palm facing us in an abhaya mudra—a gesture of assurance that grants us the blessing of fearlessness. He usually sits on His mount, a mouse.

All Hindu rituals and sacraments begin with an invocation to Lord Ganesh.

Nachiket: 'He is the Lord of New Beginnings.'

Dr Adarsh: 'Shirish and I attended a lecture by Manoj Chalam in the US a few years ago. Chalam called Lord Ganesh a "threshold deity"—an entrance to a new journey.'[53]

Lopamudra: 'He holds a lasso in one hand to pull us into His magic and enchant us. And having pulled us in, He places hurdles in our path.'

Dr Adarsh: '*Places* them? Removes them, you mean. He's *Vigneshwara* (Lord of Obstacles).[54] If there is an obstacle, whatever its nature, one can go to Him. There is no need to go to anyone else. Lord Ganesh putting obstacles in anyone's path is sounding inappropriate to me. Isn't it out of context?'

Lopamudra: 'There's no set context in Hinduism, Adarsh. It is an exploration, a search. All that matters is authentic bona fides. No mala fide intent. I have used the word "magic" also, in this context. Even this word has acquired a negative connotation. But I am plugging into the enchantment of it all. And, Lord Ganesh represents wisdom and grounding. He is not a service provider. Why would He remove your obstacles? Don't you think He has better things to do?'

Dr Adarsh: 'But He is *Vignaharta* (*Remover of Obstacles*). He is *Vignavinashanaya* (*Destroyer of Obstacles*).[55] I don't understand what you are saying, Aunty.'

Anirban: 'Neither do I. All Gods protect their followers and grant boons. This statement is sounding strange to me. What kind of God would make my life more difficult?'

Dharma Raj: 'He can be an obstacle remover also, don't worry. We can believe what we need to. Does He place them *or* remove them; does He place them *and* remove them; does He place them and expect *you* to remove them?'

Lopamudra: 'What *are* these obstacles, you think? Are they the events and happenings in our lives? Are they the confusion, misery and chaos that these events arouse within us? Are they the emotional drama that we sometimes make of our lives? Are they the challenges in our lives or our *reaction* to these challenges?'

Nachiket: 'Some people are miserable regardless of circumstances. Others have life hitting them relentlessly with pain, and yet they seem in control. What *are* these obstacles? What is the correct answer, Papa?'

Dharma Raj: 'There's no correct or incorrect answer. Just try to remember the goal of self-understanding and self-discovery. Maybe our limitations are our real obstacles. We need to overcome them, and Lord Ganesh is the gentle face of wisdom who can guide us.'

Nachiket: 'He's certainly unhurried. He sits on top of the scurrying mouse—our scurrying thoughts. We may think He is there to ease our journey. In which case, He may lower the crossbar we must jump over. We may know He is there to challenge. If so, He will raise the crossbar. The more we overcome with ease, the higher He may raise His tests.'

Lopamudra: 'Well put, Nachiket. Challenges are opportunities. Some people are defeated by life's smallest problems. Others remain strong even while everything is falling apart.'

Dr Adarsh: 'I like your interpretation of the lasso in His hand, Aunty.'

Gargi: 'The noose with which He pulls our ego and brings it under His influence ...'[56]

Nachiket: 'Fling the noose on yourself. And experience true power within you. Exercise strength over your impulses. Do not allow the centrifugal forces of life to scatter you ... at least not too often. Learn the ultimate art of leadership. Lead yourself.'

Gargi: 'Wow, Nachiket. Wow. Wow. Wow.'

Nachiket looked at her and smiled.

Dr Adarsh: 'And the laddoo is auspicious. Lord Ganesh is telling us to begin our journey with His offering.'

Nachiket: 'Not to forget, the journey is always inward. With the axe, He wants us to chop off the compulsive pull of our ego, which makes us posture and rationalize. And His fourth hand reassures us and showers us with His blessings.'

Gargi: 'His imploring eyes—it is as if He is begging us to walk on that road signposted "Character development". For which the primary *vighna* (*obstacle*) is our inflated self-image.'

Anirban: 'Sounds wonderful, but why would God beg?'

Gargi: 'Okay. He is persuading us. Inviting us, encouraging us, prompting us ... Anirban, you look at God from an Abrahamic lens—where God is the parent and the worshipper is the child. The Abrahamic God protects, rewards and punishes. He—only a He, mind you—gives us the rules, the dos and don'ts, and often the worshipper is good only because they are looking for approbation and rewards. They're collecting points that will take them to heaven and keep them away from hell. The Dharmic approach is different. God can be a friend or even an enemy. Gandhari cursed Lord Krishna after the Great Battle in Mahabharata when all her sons were dead. She blamed Lord Krishna, the God. And *cursed* Him. And the Lord accepted her curse with respect. Even after Lord Bal Gopal showed Yashoda Ma His *Vishvarupa*, she continued to chide, scold and punish her child as she deemed fit. She did not start treating Him like a God. Sage Narada once cursed Lord Vishnu, and Rishi Durvasa was famous for his anger—even against the Gods.'

Sage Narada sits in a difficult ritual penance one day. It settles deep and his dhyana will not break. The insecure Lord Indra, king of the Devas and also God of Lightning and Thunder, begins to create hurdles in Sage Narada's path. *His attention must be broken*, Lord Indra thinks. He even recruits the services of Lord Agni, God of Fire, Lord Vayu, God of the Wind, Lord Varuna, God of Water and the Seas, and Lord Madana, God of Love, in this endeavour.

He is determined to not let Sage Narada complete his penance and attain strength. Alas, they collectively fail. On completing his rigour, a pleased Sage Narada visits

Lord Vishnu, the Sustainer of the Universe, and boasts at length about his success.

Lord Vishnu silently decides to teach the sage a lesson in humility one day.

Time rolls on. Sage Narada falls in love with Shrimati, the beautiful daughter of King Shilanidhi. He requests Lord Vishnu to make Him as handsome as Hari, the Lord's most beautiful form. Lord Vishnu promises to help. However, on the assigned day He makes the sage look like Hari, the monkey. Shrimati bursts into laughter when she sees him.

Furious, Sage Narada curses Lord Vishnu that He will be separated from His beloved one day. The curse comes true when Lord Vishnu and His consort, Goddess Laxmi, descend to earth as their avatars, Lord Ram and Goddess Sita.

Sometimes intended lessons go awry, even for the Gods. They pay the price.[57]

Lord Krishna and His wife, Goddess Rukmini, invite Rishi Durvasa to their resplendent palace in Dwaraka for a meal. Rishi Durvasa accepts the invitation, but on one condition: the couple must pull the chariot themselves, ride to his ashram and escort him home. The king and queen are happy to oblige. They reach the rishi's ashram and pick him up in their royal chariot.

Halfway back home, Goddess Rukmini turns to Her husband and reveals that She is thirsty. The chariot-pulling has tired Her. Lord Krishna brings the chariot to a halt and shoots an arrow into the ground. Instantly a gurgling stream springs to the surface. Goddess Rukmini rushes forward and slakes Her thirst, without seeking the rishi's permission. The volatile Rishi Durvasa loses his temper. After all, he is their revered guest! Lord Krishna cajoles him with all His charm and seemingly manages to placate him. They continue on their journey home. On reaching the palace it is obvious to the royal couple that the sulking rishi has not let go of his anger.

Rishi Durvasa refuses to eat or drink anything. He declares that by drinking water without his permission and without sharing it with him, Goddess Rukmini insulted him and Lord Krishna condoned the insult. He curses the Lord and His consort. Goddess Rukmini henceforth will stay away from the palace. She will be separated from Her Lord and She will remain thirsty. And Lord Krishna's kingdom, Dwaraka, will be bereft of potable water.[58]

In Dwaraka stands the beautiful Dwarakadheesh Mandir of Lord Krishna. Goddess Rukmini, His beloved wife, does not stand beside Him. Her temple stands two kilometres away, distant from Her partner. Devotees to this day kindly offer a pot of water to their beloved thirsty Goddess.

Anirban: 'Hmmm. Okay.'

Dr Adarsh: 'Coming back to the ego—our inflated self-image—being the biggest obstacle. That's an interesting idea. That the obstacles we face in life are never really out there, in external life; they're within us. They're *vrittis*.[59] Fluctuations of the mind. Also, I remember my mother telling me once that Lord Ganesh has been called both Vighnaharta and Vighnakarta[60] in the *Yajnavalkya Smriti*. It makes sense now, doesn't it?'

Nachiket: 'Isn't Lord Ganesh also known as the Lord of Karma?'

Gargi: 'Oh, so the obstacles are karma?'

Dharma Raj: 'Karma is quite the omnibus term, isn't it? It has also been defined as the compulsive cycles of thought and emotional patterns that afflict us. In that sense, yes, karma is obstacles. We call them "sanchit karma". Our ability to remove them is also karma—this being active karma, which we call "agami karma". Lord Ganesh helps, but the responsibility is ours.'

Gargi: 'Opportunity too. Why not see the "obstacle" as the sweet laddoo of opportunity? Through it, we can grow, become better versions of ourselves, live life more deeply ... even understand the true meaning of life.'

Lopamudra: 'Sounds nice in theory, but it's tough to practise. Very tough. Life's challenges can drain the strongest people.'

Gargi: 'Emotions are the biggest challenge for me, not events so much.'

Lopamudra: 'Events trigger emotions. But you can separate the two if you try. Actually, stressful events trigger the underlying temperament—the tendencies and impulses. Either the animal or the child in you kicks in. Conscious character gets pushed to the backseat. Temperament is like the child, and character is the adult. Character helps us become masters and not slaves to our emotions. Character can help us use our emotions fruitfully and grow.'

Nachiket: 'And we all have a child in us. So Lord Ganesh can attract those who engage with karma and character building. What about those who are deeply entangled with emotions and are unable to master and channel them but are ruled by them?'

Lopamudra: 'For them there's Goddess Durga. Mind you, I'm not talking about surface, frothy emotions like irritation and frustration. This Mother Goddess is for those people whose feelings swim in deep waters—like insecurity, fear, guilt, anger, desire, envy and so on.'

Gargi: 'Anger, fear, *insecurity*? But She's a beautiful lady. Maybe you mean Goddess Kali.' Gargi sounded unusually defensive. She loved Goddess Durga, and saw herself as fearless and confident.

Lopamudra: 'Goddess Kali is different; She's overwhelming. Not anger—rage. Not fear—terror.

Not insecurity—desperate aloneness and despair. Not desires—addictions, compulsive addictions. However, Goddess Kali is also transformational. Let us come back to Her when we discuss Her partner, Lord Shiva.'

Anirban: 'Terror, despair, addictions ... almost too much to dwell upon. But, no doubt, Goddess Durga is beautiful.'

Dharma Raj: 'And, Her names symbolize Her mastery over the emotions we are discussing. She is called Chandika, the fierce one; Ghorarupa, the one with a fearsome appearance; Karaali, the one who is fearsome; Raudra, the one who roars; Ugra, the one who is intensely fearsome. The names indicate Her relationship with anger and fear.

'She is both Bhayada and Abhayada: the one who raises fear and the one who raises productivity and fearlessness. She is the ruler of emotions that are difficult to reach, fathom and control. She is also called Dhriti, the one who is firm and resolute. With firmness and resolution one masters insecurity. And, above all, She is beautiful.'

Mahishasur,[61] the buffalo-demon, is blessed with the boon of invincibility, which fills him with pride and arrogance. He speedily becomes a menace to life on earth. The entire army of Gods/Devas wage a battle against him but fail to overpower him. At their wits' end, they hit upon a novel plan. Why not pool their individual powers and fashion a unique and powerful Goddess? Each God bequeaths their best weapon, ability, skill and power. And thus, Goddess Durga is born.

She rides a ferocious lion and defeats the mighty Mahishasur. She is Aigiri Nandini, the darling daughter of the Mountain. She is Mahishasur-mardini, the slayer of Mahishasur!

Goddess Durga, a form of the Mother Goddess, is commonly depicted with ten hands, riding a tiger or a lion. Each hand holds a tool. Some hands hold weapons, like a bow, trident, sword, axe and mace. One hand holds a conch, another a chakra and another a lotus flower.

The *Bhagavata Purana* describes Her nine forms, popularly known as Nava Durgas—Shailaputri, Brahmacharini, Chandraghanta, Kushmanda, Skandamata, Katyayani, Kalaratri, Mahagauri and Siddhidatri.

Gargi: 'Isn't She beautiful, Goddess Durga? Her face is so calm. But She rides a ferocious lion and Her numerous hands hold so many weapons.'

Anirban: 'Also other things, yes? A conch, a chakra, a lotus flower ...'

Dr Adarsh: 'Right. How do *you* know that?'

Anirban: 'I don't know. We absorb these pictures as we grow up, I suppose.'

Dr Adarsh: 'Her weapons kill demons of course. So, who are these demons? They can't possibly be our ill-wishers.'

Dharma Raj: 'It is all relative. *You* may be the ill-wisher for *your* ill-wishers. The Goddess does not have a special interest in you. Or maybe, She does. But this special interest is in everyone. Everyone is special to Her.'

Anirban: 'Ha! True. So then? Who are the demons?'

Lopamudra: 'Could these demons be some aspect of *you*, Her devotee? The deity can serve as a mirror. Could She be reflecting me killing the demons that exist within me?'

Anirban: 'Which aspect of me do the weapons kill? How do we recognize our demons?'

Dharma Raj: 'Good question, Anirban. Difficult to answer. We must learn to answer these questions for ourselves.'

Lopamudra: 'She can acquaint us with our *svabhava*, *samskaras*, and *vaasanas*—*temperament*, *tendencies* and *subtle disposition*. Not mentally, mind you, but through a flood-like expression of these urges and a vivid outpouring of the emotions. They rise to the surface.'

Nachiket: 'Without expressing it you cannot know it. And when you do not want to know these "checking and urging forces"—as Freud calls them—you can pretend they don't exist within you, and if at all they emerge, it is someone else's fault. Till your anger or sadness ambushes you without a rationalizing escape hatch, when you least expect them to.'

Dharma Raj: 'You cannot transform yourself unless you first see yourself—fearlessly. Brutally uncover yourself in your own eyes. It is the only way true dignity and grace can find expression. Do not supress your tendencies. Channel them, recognize and become aware of them and then transform them. Have the courage to allow your nature to have its way, but with the responsibility of an adult, not the ignorant freedom of a child. Go with the flow. But channel the flow with the clarity of intention.'

Lopamudra: 'If intrinsic, unconscious tendencies are not allowed expression, they find an outlet through perversions. So let them flow, but be in control. It will help you recognize yourself. And yes, then transform yourself. Find the courage. Live consciously. That's it.'

Gargi looked at her husband. He was looking at her.

Are you telling me something?

Are you listening? Can you love all of me? Or just my best version?

Anirban laughed out loud. 'That's it, huh, Aunty?'

Nachiket: 'I see my ambushing-self often enough. How do I transform that part of me? It just takes over the driver's seat.'

Dharma Raj looked at Nachiket with piercing, keen eyes. Gargi thought she saw a hint of pride in those eyes. Befuddled, she smiled nonetheless.

Lopamudra: 'For that you need another deity. The transformer God. But you have to wait for that. Right now, we're discussing the emergence of tendencies. Unless they rise to the surface and you see them and reflect upon them, transformation is impossible.'

Dr Adarsh: 'Our addictive patterns of behaviour[62]... We usually don't even recognize these patterns in ourselves.'

Nachiket: 'But others around us do.'

Lopamudra: 'That means nothing. It's not their business. They're better off grappling with their own *samskaras*.'

Nachiket: 'Well said, Ma.'

Lopamudra: 'It's so easy to turn our gaze towards others and judge them. It's our greatest misfortune, actually.'

Dr Adarsh: 'Should we only judge ourselves?'

Nachiket: 'No. I must try and not judge myself. I must accept myself. My worst version as well. Like a mother accepts her child, and then steers her child. My worst version needs my maximum help and guidance.'

Anirban: 'That's very convenient. Shouldn't I first judge myself objectively to know what is right or wrong? Only then will I know what to steer in which direction. And while steering, accept myself. I think judging is important. Without judging, I will not know where to start. Not judging will lead to a bloated self-opinion. Judging myself is the first step to accepting myself. If I don't judge, I will not know my good and bad versions so how will I know where to start working?'

Nachiket: 'This is true for conscious behaviour, Anirban. This is true for that part of my personality that I know and am familiar with. That I can recognize. But there's more to us. I'm talking about that part in us that ambushes us, surprises us, makes us tell people, "I'm sorry, I don't know where that came from." We don't know that part in us. And we will never really know it, till we see its face.'

Dharma Raj: 'Anirban, even the part of our personality that we are aware of can be handled with *viveka* (*discernment*) and *karuna* (*compassion*). It doesn't necessarily require stern judgement, although that too can work. Judging also brings admonitions, and well-dones, nos, dont's and shouldn'ts. We can impose rules on ourselves, yes. Competently judging and steering our conduct helps us please others and ourselves and live skilfully. A careful person may detect an inconsistency in what he says and does and can reflect upon his conduct and make steady progress. Self-instructions can be stern or mild.

'But there's more to the story of human growth and possibilities than good conduct. There are aspects in us, which, if we are honest with ourselves, we cannot predict or understand. These are our unconscious, compulsive patterns. They are our motives and feelings that lurk below our thoughts. Let's call it that little child within me. It can drive me to despair, make me ashamed. Make me scared of being outed. That child in me hides inside because it does not like being judged. It might even be scared of being judged, making it run away and hide. It blocks itself from my awareness. I don't want to see it; acknowledge it. I'd much rather rationalize my bad behaviour, blame others ... When we are kind and understanding towards this disruptive, rowdy, wild, sometimes ugly child, it peeps out and shows its face. We must own that child in us. Pick it up in our arms, so to speak. Embrace it, soothe it, then teach it appropriateness and rectify it.'

Nachiket: 'This is when you find true self-love and self-acceptance. When you choose to love that frightened, alarmed or angry child instead of making it feel ignored and increasing its ferocity. So that it calms down. It needs feminine energy from me. It needs to feel accepted and owned.'

Gargi looked at Nachiket furtively, then quickly looked away. Nachiket pretended not to notice the movement.

Dharma Raj: 'Till then, it hides in plain sight. Others see it but you don't. Those who love you see it more often and even suffer the brunt of it, while you are busy blaming others or rationalizing your occasional conduct ... Try and not judge anybody. Instead, try and understand, with kindness. And begin with yourself.

Learn to observe yourself with detachment, as if you are someone else. Be aware. Don't identify too much with yourself. Or too little. Both will blur your vision and fill you with excuses ...'

Lopamudra: 'Judging keeps us clueless about this beast within us. And then the dam bursts and this unhappy, sometimes mean and malevolent beast breaks out. Goddess Durga and Goddess Kali can help this child emerge so that we can see it—Goddess Durga for the suffering child, Goddess Kali for the bitter or hostile child. Why do you think Goddess Durga holds all these weapons?'

Gargi: 'Tell us, Ma.'

Lopamudra: 'Because temperament is like the Greek water-monster Hydra, with multiple heads. It is persistent and unpredictable. It is sly and difficult to overpower. We need the entire armoury. And we need to be heroic.'

Hydra is a water-serpent with nine heads that lives in the swamps of Lerna. It emerges at will and harasses the livestock and humans. The people are scared, for it is invincible. If one head is lopped off, it grows two more.

Hercules, the iconic hero, comes to the rescue. He lops off each head and cauterizes the stump with a burning torch. The last immortal head remains. Hercules slices it and cauterizes the wound. And then buries the head under a gigantic rock, never to rise again.[63]

Gargi: 'Is temperament always negative? Some of it can be positive, *na*? I'm just wondering.'

Dharma Raj: 'Your wondering is valid. Temperament is formed by different kinds of unconscious memories—genetic memory, evolutionary memory, cell memory, foetal memory. And, of course, early childhood memory. These memories do not exist at the level of words, so whether "positive" or "negative", they're unconscious. We are not consciously aware of this part of ourselves.'

Lopamudra: 'Either way, developing our character will overwrite the parts of our temperament that need to be erased or modified, and enhance those parts which are beautiful. It is a very conscious effort. If we're lucky, Goddess Durga will help us recognize our deepest fears, desires, ambitions, and secret yearnings. They're all buried under automatic and habitual patterns of emotions and thoughts. They're very compelling. These are things we do automatically, without thinking. It is taken for granted that we will behave in this manner and we usually do not evaluate or review these actions. These tendencies are the primary drivers of our non-public conduct. How we behave when no one is watching, or when only the people we take for granted are watching. They get ingrained in our personality as we grow older.'

Anirban: 'I like that—non-public conduct. The person I really am—in my home, with my family, when I'm alone. Also, with strangers or people who make no difference to me.'

Dharma Raj: 'When we are with strangers, we feel we are alone.'

Lopamudra: 'We will gradually recognize that Goddess Durga does not fight our battles or satisfy our yearnings. In fact, these challenges do not lie in external life at all. When we're ready, the Goddess pours Her strength into us. And we're able to defeat the demons inside us and silence them.'

Gargi: 'And if we're not ready?'

Nachiket: 'Then She continues to pull us towards Her. Again and again.'

Lopamudra: 'She draws out the muck. She makes us cry. It could be grief, exasperation, anger, fear or helplessness. It could be reproach, desire or anxiety. She makes us laugh deliriously or flay in frustration. We scold, we plead, we ache. We feel alone and abandoned. We swim in the tidal waves of emotions.'

Dr Adarsh: 'We may even feel temporarily assuaged. My Ma has kept *mannats* all her life for Goddess Durga. Fulfilling them gives her great satisfaction.'

Anirban: 'So what exactly are these *mannats* or *maantas*? My *ammamma* (*grandmother*) was a great believer in them. I think it's a pathetic attempt at bribing the Gods. Silly.'

Dharma Raj smiled. 'The *Satyanarayan katha* is in a similar vein. We can call it a carrot-and-stick approach to good behaviour or we can try and understand the human need for solace, Anirban.'

A rich merchant and his wife—seth and sethani—are childless and desperately crave a little one. A well-wisher advises them to conduct the *Satyanarayan katha* ritual and their wish will be granted. 'Be warned,' the friend advises, 'that you conduct the ritual on twelve nights of the full moon.'

The couple conduct the ceremony on a full moon night and, lo and behold, Leelavati, the sethani, conceives soon thereafter. A bonny daughter is born nine months later to great rejoicing. They name her Kalavati. The seth gets busy with trade affairs and forgets his resolve to conduct the *Satyanarayan katha*.

Time flies, and Kalavati has grown into a beautiful and accomplished young girl. Peace prevails but the sethani is haunted by the unkept promise and reminds her husband that they must conduct the ritual, lest their daughter suffers the consequences. He promises that he will conduct the katha as one of the ceremonies when Kalavati marries.

The fond parents find a suitable match for Kalavati and marry her off with pomp and splendour, and yet no *Satyanarayan katha* is conducted. The patient Lord Narayan finally decides to teach the merchant a lesson in translating intention into action and the consequences of absence of attention. It is time for the seth to learn the value of commitment.

The seth sets off by ship on a trade visit accompanied by his young and sprightly son-in-law. Meanwhile, some thieves loot the palace of King Chandraketu and some making a quick getaway they hide the loot at the *vishram sthal* (*resthouse*) where the duo is staying. The king mistakenly arrests the hapless men. The women pray for their release. The Lord gives the king a *sakshatkar* (*an appearance*) and the men are released.

Having concluded a successful trip, the two men are on their way home, their boat heavy with the wealth they have earned. Then, Lord Narayan tests them. He approaches them in the garb of a poor old man and asks for alms. The seth tells Him that they have nothing in the boat. Lord Narayan says, '*Tathastu. (So be it.*)' And, the boat lightens with the weight of nothing!

The seth recognizes Lord Narayan and is immediately contrite. He begs forgiveness and profusely promises that he will conduct the katha when he reaches home.

Meanwhile Leelavati, the sethani, and Kalavati, her daughter, decide to conduct the katha while the men are away. As the katha draws to a close they receive news that the seth and his son-in-law have reached the riverbank. The excited women leave the seat of ritual and rush out to greet the men. The women too need a lesson in discipline, Lord Narayan decides.

When they reach the riverbank, they find no boat. It has sunk, they are told by onlookers. The women sink to the ground and break into loud wails. And then they hear the *akashvani* (*message from the sky*):

These two women left the ceremony incomplete. The prasad of the Lord lay unreceived. They were doing well. They were fulfilling their charter. Why did they lose attention towards the end of the ceremony?

The women go back home and respectfully eat the prasad. They complete the ritual and make their way back to the riverbank. To their amazement they find their husbands unscathed, unharmed. All return home and thank the Lord.[64]

Truth, attention and form are re-established.

Dr Adarsh: 'A *maanta* or *vrata* is an action we intend to carry out or an austerity we maintain till a wish is fulfilled by the Gods. Many such *vratas* are directed to the Goddess. My mother abstains from some type of food or drink for long periods of time.'

Lopamudra: 'You call it solace, Raj. Solace is temporary. Your mother would use another word for the *Satyanarayan katha*. *Sateek* (*appropriate*). She was convinced it was a most appropriate katha for the times we live in. The *Satyanarayan katha* is fundamentally a tale of commitment and consequences. To make commitments with consciousness and know that unkept commitments have consequences. Accept them. But, of course, unless we learn to identify the basis and origin of our thinking and feeling patterns, we act them out again and again.'

Dharma Raj: 'Even if it is for a few moments, solace is critical. It may be all that a person wants, or even needs, at that time. We can only identify the basis and origin of our patterns if that frightened child inside us feels safe. And the Goddess is persistent. She squeezes out the emotional *tute hue tukde* (*broken pieces*) and brings them to the surface again and again. We can keep removing them from the stack, one after another, till we reach the one trauma that went in first. And the Goddess waits ...'

Gargi: '*Tute hue tukde.*'

Dharma Raj: 'Yes. Sounds harsh, but that is what it is.'

Nachiket: 'You say the Goddess waits. For what?'

Dharma Raj: 'For you to find your inner strength. And begin your journey towards even-mindedness. Unbroken tranquillity and joy.'

Lopamudra: 'The root of the word "vrata" is "vru", to choose. Are you choosing to be a slave to your wishes and impulses? To empower your fears and whims? Or are you choosing to transform?'

Dharma Raj: 'If it's transformation you're seeking ...'

Gargi: 'What if you're not seeking transformation? What if you're happy the way you are?'

Dharma Raj: 'That's fine. You can leave transformation for later. But you'll get to that stage eventually. If not as Gargi, then as someone else—in the next life. It is the soul's journey. For now, it's enough to blow the conch and say, "Jai Mata Di!"'

11

ADI YOGI,
THE FIRST YOGI

'Let's play some music.' Gargi got up and walked into the house before anyone could respond. A few minutes later, she came out with a portable speaker and synced her phone with it.

Gargi: 'What would you like to listen to?'

Nachiket: 'Now that you give us the choice …' Gargi narrowed her eyes as she looked at her husband, then scrunched her nose and smiled. Nachiket held her gaze indulgently.

Lopamudra: 'Should we play the "Atma Shatakam"?'

Anirban: 'What's that?'

Lopamudra: 'You probably know it as "Shivohum Shivohum". It is said to have been composed by Adi Shankaracharya[65].'

Gargi: 'Or wait, let me play something joyful and lively. Raga Yaman[66], Papa? I hope it's not too scandalous to talk while Yaman plays in the background.'

Lopamudra: 'So long as you don't play a Shree or a Marva. They demand attention. They're serious ragas. Raga Shree is associated with devotion and dedication, and Raga Marwa is contemplative, even melancholic[67].'

Dharma Raj: '... *Nishadachi hurhoor dakhavnara, rishabhache aakrandan karnara aani shadjacha aasra shodhnara toe marva!* Pu. La. Deshpande...'

Nachiket: '*That Marva! After expressing the apprehensive anxiety of Nishad and the bewailing Rishabh, it seeks refuge in Shadja ...*'

Gargi: 'All right, then! Presenting Raga Yaman by Niladri Kumar.'

For fifteen minutes, the fluid plucking of the sitar seemed to decorate the sound of silence. It filled the air with joy. The evening subtly transformed.

Anirban: 'Uncle, you were talking about transformation—the God who transforms.'

Dharma Raj did not open his eyes.

Lopamudra: 'If it's time for transformation, then it's time for the Lord of the Lords—Mahadev—Lord Shiva. You will find that your *Ishta Devata* too might change when you're ready for transformation, and you will begin to feel a pull towards the Mahadev. As you change through life, your *Ishta Devata* subtly changes.'

Sage Bhringi is an ardent devotee of Lord Shiva whose mornings begin with seven circumambulations of the Lord. Always. One morning he approaches his Lord but finds His consort, Goddess Parvati, seated beside

Him. He carefully circumambulates his guru, squeezing himself between the couple so he needn't include the Lord's wife. Goddess Parvati is annoyed. The amused Lord suggests She move closer and include Herself in the obeisance.

She does. So Sage Bhringi transforms himself into a mouse and scurries in between the two. She is excluded again. Now the Lord lifts His wife and places Her on His lap but Sage Bhringi will not be outmanoeuvred. He transforms into a little bird and flies around his Lord, excluding the Goddess again. She fumes, and He gathers Her close and makes Her a part of Him. They meld, half-and-half, into one another. They are *Ardhanarishwar* now—part-masculine, part-feminine.

Sage Bhringi will not relent. He transforms himself into a bee and buzzes around the right side. Lord Shiva knows it's time for His great devotee to understand the true nature of existence. Shiva, the Lord of Yoga, sits in siddhasana. It allows no space between the two legs. Bhringi can see that he must honour the feminine and masculine impulse, without separation. He does.[68]

In modern times, Lord Shiva is often called the 'destroyer' among the Hindu trinity of Gods. This is, perhaps, an inadequate understanding. More appropriately, He is the transformer, for nothing gets destroyed in the universe; it only changes form. A multifaceted being, He is the ascetic who is also a skilled dancer and musician, a householder who is the patron God of yoga. He is a disruptor but has also created basic Sanskrit grammar.

He is worshipped in the iconic form of the Shivalinga and as a householder. He sits beside His consort, Goddess Parvati, while His children, Lord Ganesh and Lord Kartikeya, sit on His lap. As mentioned earlier, in North India, Lord Ganesh is the younger child, whereas in South India, Lord Ganesh is the older one. Lord Kartikeya is a celibate for North Indians, whereas South Indians believe He has two wives, Valli and Sena.

As the yogi in contemplation, Lord Shiva has Vasuki, the king of snakes, wrapped around His neck. A crescent moon sits on His head, which accords Him the name Chandramauli. With the cool, disciplined mind of a yogi, He symbolizes the silencing of emotions. The two eyes that perceive are closed, for He has turned within in contemplation. Lord Shiva is intuition. The sixth sense. He sees what the two eyes do not see.

Planted beside Him is a *trishul* (*trident*). It represents the three gunas—*sattva*, *rajas* and *tamas*. These gunas represent our unique nature. Tied to the trident is a *damaru* (*pellet drum*); Shiva is rhythm and order. Each of us must find the rhythmic life that suits our nature and bring the gunas into balance. Step by step.

Shiva is Aum. It is believed that Aum was the first sound of the universe. Sound energy emerges from movement and physics educates us that nothing is static in the universe, everything vibrates. And when movement acquires rhythm, there is order.

Lord Shiva is the householder who is also *bairagi* (*ascetic recluse*). He drinks bhang, an intoxicant, and is also Adi Yogi, the originator of Yoga, which is a path to physical, mental, emotional and spiritual balance. He prefers coarse, even macabre companions and at the same time is a lesson in nobility in the manner He treats His wife. He symbolizes renunciation but the sensual love He shares with His wife is the stuff of lore. He is an anti-elitist God, always on the side of the disempowered, dispossessed and those on the fringe. And, at the same time, He is the originator of many art forms, beloved of the elite; even as He wears clothes that would be unacceptable in polite society: a tiger-skin skirt with ash smeared on His naked torso. He is *Nataraj* (*Lord of Dance*). And He dances with His ghoulish friends in cremation ghats. He is a repository of contradictions.

Lord Shiva represents the potential in us to achieve balance, beauty, rhythm, order and self-mastery through transformation.

Dharma Raj: 'Transformation is internal, and an essential first step for it is confusion. Lord Shiva is the Lord of Contradictions. He confuses and confounds. He is alert attention. But He also provokes. He excites. Lord Shiva can lead you completely astray sometimes. But there is purpose in that too.'

Lopamudra: 'Going astray can give you the opportunity to see yourself. Lord Shiva can make the real you emerge from its darkness and the shadows where it lurks. He makes you stop fooling yourself. And makes you want to change.'

Gargi: 'Doesn't that sound like what was earlier discussed about Goddess Durga?'

Lopamudra smiled. 'Spiritual paths lead to the same goal. Self-understanding, self-mastery and then growth towards fulfilling our potential. Inner integration and then external integration with life. Achieving internal harmony within ourselves and external harmony with all life is the goal. Different strokes work for different folks. Each person resonates with a different frequency, connecting them to different Chosen Gods and Goddesses. Remember we said it is inexplicable, the pull. Like falling in love, and there are subtle differences. Goddess Durga can bring pain, anger, hurt, yearning and fear to the surface.[69] Goddess Kali can bring rage, despair, terror, injuries, outrage and rancour to the surface.[70] You really can get stuck with these two, so beware!'

Dharma Raj: 'The key thing you said, Lopa, was that Lord Shiva can make you stop fooling yourself when you see what lies underneath the masks of rationalizations, analyses and blaming. He brings our contradictions and paradoxes to the surface. And when they become impossible to ignore, you transform.'

Nachiket: 'So, Lord Shiva begins to pull when we come to the end of the road with Goddesses Durga and Kali. *If* and when we reach the end of that road.'

Lopamudra: 'Or, He can join that road. Especially with Goddess Kali. Remember, She is the Goddess of Transformation. Alone She rages and is outraged. Lord Shiva quietens Her and together they can transform.'

Goddess Durga has vanquished Mahishasur, the buffalo-demon. She now takes on the fierce Asura Raktabija, but the demon proves invincible for the mighty Goddess. Having invoked the blessings of Lord Brahma, with every injury the drops of his blood that fall to the ground eerily give rise to innumerable duplicate Raktabijas. It is a fierce impasse.

Goddess Kali is summoned to control the situation. Taking charge, She devours the demon and all his duplicates, without a single drop of blood falling to the ground. But now She is enraged. She is consumed by bloodlust. Goddess Kali goes on a rampage and kills multiple other demons. As Chamunda, She slays the demons Chanda and Munda. The fierce Goddess is unstoppable and the havoc She creates now threatens the stability of the cosmos. The Gods approach Her, one by one, but are unable to pacify Her. Lord Vishnu steps up, but He too fails to quieten the bloodthirsty Goddess. They make their way to the silent Lord Shiva, Her consort. Lord Shiva lays down on the ground and the ferocious Goddess mistakenly steps on Her consort. Horrified, She instantly stills and sticks Her tongue out with regret and alarm. The horror ceases.

She transforms and becomes the still and beautiful Goddess Gauri.

Goddess Kali is the darkest form of Goddess Parvati. She is the fierce Mother Goddess, the embodiment of destruction and also fierce compassion. She destroys only to renew and transform. She can invoke fear and awe. She is both Ugra Kali, the raging Goddess, and Deepta Kali, the one who illuminates. She captures dread and transforms it into compassion and understanding. If we integrate the darkness within us, we become aware.

She is Charunetra, the one with beautiful eyes, and Kameshwari, the queen of desire. She instils fear if we are afraid, and insight and compassion if we embrace Her transformational possibilities. From suffering emerges the illumination of understanding.

Goddess Kali is the fiercest form of the Mother Goddess. She is worshipped as the ultimate reality in the Kaula School of Tantric Shaivism. Mahakali is Her ten-handed form, while Bhadrakali is a milder form. Dakshinakali and Vamakali are tantric forms of the Goddess.

As Bengalis, proud worshippers of the Mother Goddess frequently exclaim, *'Shobi Maaer ichhey!* (*All is Ma's wish!*)[71]'

Gargi: 'I'll settle for that. You guys were making me question myself for getting attracted to Goddesses Durga and Kali. I'm a joyful person, thank you!'

Dharma Raj: 'It is impossible to ignore Goddess Kali. She personifies destruction and mayhem. She drinks the blood of Her combatants. Shambhavi Chopra calls Her imagery fierce and yet, also calls Her "reassuring in her blessings in the way of sympathy or compassion".[72] Sadhguru calls Lord Shiva "Mahakala, the Lord of Time", while Maha Kali is His "female counterpart ... Destruction becomes the foundation of a new creation" in Time.'[73]

Gargi: 'Fierce compassion. Light emerges from darkness ...'

Lopamudra: 'Lord Shiva works really well with the fringes of society and people at the extremes. Those who don't tread the beaten path or live by some agreed rules of society. At both ends—the geniuses and innovators as well as those who drop out of normative living.'

Anirban: 'So, if the Americans were idol-worshippers, then Lord Shiva could be the God of the American biker gangs and rock groups! Why is He called the Lord of Contradictions?'

Gargi: 'It's obvious, Anirban. He's ash-smeared and not exactly a natty dresser. But He's also the Master of the arts and beauty. He dabbles in intoxicants but He's Adi Yogi, the founder of the path to health, wellness and equanimity.'

Dharma Raj: 'He is both an ascetic and a happy householder. A yogi who is also an erotic lover. You should learn Sanskrit just so you can read Kalidas's *Kumarasambhava*. It would astound the most passionate liberal of our times.'

Gargi: 'Ma called Him "Bholenath", the innocent. But His fury strikes terror in people's hearts. How can innocence be terrifying?'

Anirban: 'Here comes the attack, Gargi. You have given me an opening. You have taken two unlinked traits, put them together and created a question. It may sound intellectual but it has no meaning. Let me explain ... Aunty called Him Bholenath, the innocent. For instance, with complete respect, I say that innocence cannot have three eyes. Or, that innocence cannot dance. These are unconnected traits. Your statement means nothing.'

Gargi: 'Okay, buddy. I choose to say it again: how can innocence be terrifying? And I differentiate this from your statement, with this counter. Innocence cannot terrify but innocence can or cannot have three eyes. Remember the tuatara in New Zealand? There must surely be some among them that are innocent, some not! What about the Chinese Erlang Shen with three eyes that Malivalaya once mentioned? Some images are terrifying while some Taoist ones are most benign. Innocence can choose to either dance or not dance. But, for crying out loud, innocence CANNOT terrify. Does an infant terrify you?'

Nachiket's not-innocent eyes were dancing in merriment. He looked at his father-in-law, who returned the look. Fond amusement dripped from Dharma Raj's eyes. Lopamudra was looking at Anirban quizzically.

Nachiket: 'It's all right, Ma. This is the way these two are. They enjoy their sparring. Sometimes it is nonsense.'

Anirban: 'No, Gargi, an infant does not terrify me. You do!'

Gargi laughed aloud, like only she could, her voice almost carrying to the Bhides next door.

Anirban: 'Nachiket, is she innocent?'

Nachiket: 'Mostly.'

The Chinese Goddess Yaoji rules the domain of desire in heaven and moderates the influence of greed, ambition and affection on man and woman.

One day an evil red dragon escapes its heavenly prison and descends into the world of mortals. Goddess Yaoji goes after it but is injured in the great battle with the dragon. Yang Tianyou, an erudite man on earth rescues the beautiful Goddess and nurtures Her back to health. The two fall madly in love. They have three children, their second-born being the God Erlang Shen.

Er is two, *lang* is wolf, and *shen* is God. So, He is the Two Wolf God.

God Erlang Shen has a third eye in the middle of His forehead. It is His truth-seeing eye.

He is the sage warrior who protects human beings on earth and the Gods in heaven. He slays demons and dragons. He's also the thinker and the engineer who prevents floods and devices irrigation systems to bring water to human beings.

God Erlang Shen is accompanied by Xiaotian Quan, His devoted dog who assists Him in His tasks. In the battle with Sun Wukong, the monkey king, Xiaotian Quan bites him on the leg, thus helping his master win.

Erlang Shen is the three-eyed—truth-seeing God with the true-hearted dog.[74]

Anirban: 'Just saying, Gargi ... innocence and terror can be exhibited at different moments in time.'

Gargi: 'Ooookayyyyy ... You win. Happy?'

Dharma Raj: 'Anirban, divine iconography is not about different moments so much as different levels of self-awareness. Lord Shiva is innocent and terrifying at different levels. He is ascetic and sensual at different levels. He is the embodiment of attention and also symbolic of scattered distraction at different levels. You find yourself accessing one quality, another person accesses another quality ... or you access different levels at different moments in your life. Examine what you are accessing ... and when it is Lord Shiva, notice the paradoxes within you.'

Lopamudra continued. 'He yanks us from our comfort zone and confronts us with our paradoxes. If we're able to accept and resolve them, we move towards balance and rhythm.'

Dr Adarsh: 'Things can swing in the other direction too, like Gargi said.'

Dharma Raj: 'Of course. Lord Shiva can make you go completely off-balance. You either drag yourself down or lift yourself up.'

Anirban: 'How? You are talking about a God's influence on one's mind. How will this happen? Through worship? Through devotion? What is the process? Or are you asking me to take this at face-value? Then it is belief. Faith.'

Dharma Raj: 'The allusions are symbolic, and symbols are best accessed with reflection and intuition. Lopa's and my words on the "how" would not be applicable to you because you are a completely different human being. Lopa's and my approaches too would be very different. But it can be said that symbols and mythology allude. The off-balanced as well as the balanced lean on Lord Shiva, it is said. Like the *Shivji ki baraat*, which had them all: the Devas, the ghouls, the happy, the wailing and the unhappy. Lift yourself up, as Lopa said. You try and lift yourself towards your potential, I presume. *Chidananda roopaha Shivohum Shivohum.* (*I am indeed, that eternal Knowing and Consciousness.*) Reflect upon these two concepts. And try and set your scepticism aside when you reflect. Put your heart into it.'

Gargi: 'So we can either become certified members of His "*Shivji ki baraat*", His "crazies", or we can find our Shaivic centre, stillness and composure. *Chidananda roopaha*—it is true that there is no other God or Goddess who inspires the kind of devotion, love and passion that Lord Shiva does in His devotees.'

The equanimous Lord Vishnu decides to worship Lord Shiva with 1,000 blue lotuses. For 1,000 years He prays, every day. In the morning He collects the flowers and then takes His seat of prayer. He lifts each flower with reverence and offers it to the Mahadev.

One day the Mahadev places a test—a hurdle—in Lord Vishnu's path. He steals a flower. Unaware, Lord Vishnu begins His prayer. He offers His devotion to the Lord, one careful flower at a time. He picks up the last flower. The count is 999. He discovers He is one short. Bereft, He plucks His lotus-shaped left eye and offers it to the Mahadev. The count is complete—1,000.

Moved, Lord Shiva instantly appears in form. He restores the beautiful, lotus-shaped eye and gives the Sudarshan Chakra to His great devotee. It is the revolving disc of annihilation. Heretofore, it belongs to Lord Vishnu.[75]

Lopamudra: 'Lord Shiva does have His crazy, passionate and even dark followers. Remember, even Raavan was a devotee of Lord Shiva. The Lord accepts all kinds of followers, loves them and gives them space. Some become His disciples. Some completely transform.'

Anirban: 'Aunty, I liked what you said about rhythm and balance. The solar system has rhythm; our heartbeat has rhythm. Any kind of disturbance in rhythm spells trouble.'

Dharma Raj: 'Without rhythm, there is no discipline or beauty. Also, when there's no rhythm, our thoughts and emotions are chaotic.'

Gargi: 'Actions too. It's all connected. Even our breathing must be rhythmic. When we lose rhythm, we lose energy. Basically, a non-rhythmic life becomes unbalanced.'

Anirban: 'What about the Nataraj?'

Gargi: 'What about it?'

Anirban: 'What does it say to us?'

Lopamudra: 'A lot. Where do we begin and end? We could discuss the Nataraj for the rest of the evening.'

Dharma Raj: 'Well, the Nataraj is from the *Natya Shastra*. Nataraj is Lord Shiva, the King of Dance. The Nataraj performs many iconic dances, like the Tandava. Actually, there are many Tandava dances. One of them is the Tripura Tandava dance. The Lasya dance is its counterpart.'

Tarakasura the Asura has three sons: Tarakaksha, Vidyunmali and Kamalaksha. Together the trio are called *Tripurasura (the ones who are fused together in an unbreakable bond of brotherhood)*. One morning they sit in ritual submission to Lord Brahma the Creator.

They do not stop. The terrible *tapasya* continues for thousands of years. Lord Brahma is pleased by their *penance* and grants them their desire: Tripura, the three cosmopolises. They now possess three impregnable citadels made of gold, silver and iron.

At first the brothers live in peace. A series of circumstances then breaks their bond. Entropy sets in and they lose their restraint. From their secure bases the brothers generate chaos and disorder. The Gods observe, mute, for the fortresses are impenetrable. Helpless, they turn to Lord Shiva, who engages the brothers in a battle that lasts for three days, fierce and relentless. During the face-off, Lord Mahadev's wrath increases in steady pulses as though in rhythm. Finally, it is ferocious and raw. The cities are burnt to cinders by a single weapon: Pashupatiastra. The three brothers are reduced to ash.

The impact of the collisions stays on. Excessive energy needs channelized dissipation, both in the material world and in the skittish world of emotions; especially so with the scalding energy of anger. What goes up must come down. So, now there is havoc, for Lord Shiva remains enraged. His wrath must, equally rhythmically and with discipline, dissolve and make space for calm once again. And so, He begins to dance the Tripura Tandava.[76]

His movements are firm, sharp and full of force. His vigour threatens the balance of the cosmos. It is a dance of exultation and triumph. It is a dance of rage and power. It is a consummate dance of destruction. Goddess Parvati, His consort, clearly sees that Her partner must be pacified. She rises and steps in front of Him. Femininity softly holds the masculine gaze and the Goddess begins the dance of Lasya[77]. She moves with fluid pliancy and languid grace. Her limbs blur in hypnotic circularity while unbent light melts into the sway of Her body. His anger stands in sharp contrast with Her joy and elegant beauty. His rage, He sees, is a jarring presence in Her compassion and allure.

Rhythm had given birth to melody and their joint resonance births harmony. Their masculine and feminine vibrations find balance. The Goddess leads, being the embodiment of *Shakti*. He follows and moves towards neutrality.

Masculine and feminine energies fuse into the physical form of *Ardhanarishwar*—the Half-female Lord—a symbol of the inseparability of masculine and feminine energy.[78]

Dharma Raj: 'Lord Shiva's dances represent our transformational journey. Ancient art has captured all the poses of the Tandava. There's the forceful fury of the Rudra Tandava and the unified consciousness of the Ananda Tandava. But Lopa is right. Where do we begin and where do we end with the Nataraj?'

Lopamudra: 'I suggest we restrict ourselves to Apasmara.'

Dharma Raj: 'Excellent suggestion as usual, Madam Philosopher!'

Gargi: 'Who's Apasmara?'[79]

Lopamudra: 'How carefully have you looked at the Nataraj? Have you noticed something under Lord Shiva's right foot?'

Nachiket: 'He's crushing a monster under His foot, isn't He? It must be a demon.'

Lopamudra: 'It is a demon, but not the sort you would imagine, Nachiket. "Apasmara" in Sanskrit means "lack of memory", and also refers to epilepsy[80]. The demon under Lord Shiva's foot is symbolic of the possibility of mindful memory. From accessing memory unwisely to mindful memory.'

Anirban: 'Recollection is recollection. It pops up when it will.'

Dharma Raj: 'More's the pity ... Incidentally, "smara" is "memory" in Sanskrit. And "apasmara", "the negation of memory", is also the word for epilepsy. Seizures. Adarsh, I suppose you have seen patients having epileptic attacks?'[81]

Dr Adarsh: 'I have, Uncle. Several times. The first time it happened, I was on night duty at CMC (Christian Medical College, Vellore). I was sleeping in the common room when a nurse came and woke me. It was an eight-year-old child—' Dr Adarsh felt a lump in his throat. Strange. It was as if he was back in that room, feeling the same horror.

Fear. Fascination. Even after so many years.

Dharma Raj: 'An epileptic attack disconnects the person from the world. When it is over, the patient remembers nothing. Nothing at all. It is called absence seizures. The person is absent. It is as if time does not exist for that person in those moments. I remember a Nigerian drug peddler in my lock-up whom I was interrogating once. Suddenly, he went down. His eyes rolled to the side of his forehead and he began foaming at the mouth. He lost control over his bladder and bowels ... But it was the expression on his face that shocked me. My God! The human mask had dropped.'

Everybody became silent.

Dr Adarsh: 'We humans maintain an appearance, yes. A pretty picture. Not only in public, but also in private. Very rarely does our mask drop completely. What you're saying is that in a seizure, the pretence breaks down completely. The curtain lifts. The mask is ripped off.'

Gargi: 'It is not fair to use that word—pretence. Pretence suggests intent. It's just being human, isn't it? A seizure takes away consciousness, but when you say a mask is ripped off, you make it sound like a good thing.

Like it's desirable ... Some masks are best not lifted, I would say.'

Dharma Raj: 'Absence of consciousness can never be a completely good thing. In the path of spiritual advancement, every mask must eventually lift from our vision of ourselves. It is the ultimate desire—the longing to break free of self-ignorance and reach self-realization.'

Dr Adarsh: 'The awesome power of the brain gets displayed in an epileptic attack. The primitive brain is exposed, in full view. You have no ability to control it or redirect it. You are completely hands-off in your own drama.'

Gargi: 'What do you mean by primitive brain? How exactly is the brain's power on display? I don't know ... What you say sounds compelling, but will it hold up to scrutiny?'

Dr Adarsh: 'More powerfully than you can imagine, Gargi. What I just said will hold up to the full scrutiny of science. I am talking about the physiology of the brain. The primitive brain is also known as the reptilian brain: the brain stem, cerebellum and so on. Then there is the limbic system which houses emotions, long-term memory, etc. And then there is the cerebral cortex, built on top of the primitive structures, which has the frontal, parietal, temporal and occipital lobes[82] ... There are intricate interconnections among all these parts of the brain. The temporal lobe, for instance, houses memory as well.

'Even the cerebral cortex is not fully accessible to our awareness. The primitive parts, not at all. But they affect our personality and our behaviour in a fundamental way. To the extent we are able to control, even mask, their impulses, we "pretend". But those impulses lurk underneath.'

Nachiket: 'So, the brain's power is on display when those impulses that exist in the underbelly of the brain, underneath our consciousness, are on full display.'

Dr Adarsh: 'That night in CMC ... I remember being frightened, but I just couldn't look away. I hated myself for being enthralled, but I couldn't help it.'

Anirban: 'Reminds me of Tlazolteotl[83], the Aztec fertility Goddess of Darkness and Dark Earth. She is a complex Goddess—the dark deity who presides over lust, vice and filth. Frankly I thought it was inappropriate and primitive. Goddess of Vice?!'

Dharma Raj: 'Fascinating ... Tell us more about Her.'

Anirban: 'She oversees birth and death and purifies the dying before they embark on their journey to the other side. Gamblers and adulterers gravitate towards Her. She has the power to sponge away human sins and release us from the grip of base actions; the purifier who brings vices to the surface and then forgives ...'

Dharma Raj: 'Doesn't sound primitive at all, when you also call her the purifier. How do you clean a room unless you see the filth? How do we clean ourselves unless we see what needs cleaning?'

Anirban: 'Coming back to epilepsy, do you know it was considered a sacred illness by the ancient Greeks? I am not sure why. Was it to hide their incompetence as they did not know how to cure it? So, were they attributing to God—or rather, Gods—their own failure?'

Lopamudra: 'That is what many linear progressives would like to believe. We cannot know their motives. It satisfies the arrogance of the modern man to think that the ancients knew less. Would they not have called all diseases that they could not cure sacred then? Why only this one?'

Dharma Raj: 'I like to think otherwise. Epilepsy is linked to memory, and memory is not mere recollection. The nature of our relationship with memory can be a spiritual opportunity to expand our consciousness. From unmindfully to mindfully accessing memory. Plato said, "Know thyself." Memory can be the means through which we raise our consciousness and know who we really are. Memory can make us sink into our animal self or it can lift us completely and touch the divine. If memory is only a recollection, then we would all be helpless victims of past events—victims of Apasmara, the monster. There would be no learning from the past experience or from the next experience.'

Dr Adarsh: 'It's interesting that you should say that. Epilepsy most commonly originates in the temporal lobe of the brain, and the temporal cortex is the seat of memory. Each temporal lobe has the hippocampus, shaped like a seahorse, which is like our internal DVD player. Memories—visual, auditory, olfactory, tactile—are recorded onto it, nonstop, from the time a child is born.

'Some of the strongest recordings are from when you are an infant and toddler. Dr Penfield, a neurosurgeon, did some amazing research on this in the 1950s. He concluded that any input from our sense organs is recorded in our temporal lobes in great detail. It is "played back" in the present moment when memory is aroused by triggers and we respond disproportionately to the current event, in hindsight not understanding why we behaved the way we did. The trigger transports us back to those past events. The thing is, not only the events, even the feelings associated with those events are recorded in great detail. The event and the feelings are locked together and both are activated simultaneously. Suddenly, you are transported back in time. You are in that moment, feeling the same thing—anger, fear, sadness, rage, despair or whatever. It is a reproduction of what happened earlier. Dr Penfield called it a "re-living". You are not just recollecting or remembering. You are there. You become a different person.'[84]

Dharma Raj: 'So, we relive the past intense experience by reliving the same triggered emotion ...'

Gargi's eyes widened. She discreetly looked at her husband. Her Nachiket felt all the human emotions intensely: anger, guilt, desire, love, compassion, empathy, hurt. Hurt. He did not suppress them, especially the anger that raged within him, which would only be triggered by extreme stress.

It had never frightened Gargi, this anger, as she had instinctively understood that it had nothing to do with her. She would withdraw emotionally and emerge when that anger subsided, as it invariably did. And her man was back with his self-deprecatory humour, calm, equanimity and attentive love.

He sat now like a coiled panther, ready to leap. His eyes were like knife-slits. And yet, he was still. Quiet. He felt her eyes upon him, and relaxed. His face softened.

Dr Adarsh continued: 'It's like you've travelled back in time. He called the brain a high-fidelity recorder which records every experience, possibly from even before birth. The playback is high-fidelity and these recordings are continuous and in sequence.'

Dharma Raj: 'Of course, only those things are recorded that we pay attention to, although we don't always have control over this, especially in childhood. If your father is arguing loudly with your mother or, even worse, beating her while you lie in bed in the next room, you are automatically attentive. If your mother is shouting at someone or crying disconsolately, the fear and grief are engraved in your brain through imprinting.'

Dr Adarsh: 'Dr Penfield called the temporal lobe a library with many volumes. It replays vividly when triggered. You feel the same emotions in the present moment.'

Dharma Raj: 'The past influences the present, casts a shadow over it. And that is where Nataraj and Apasmara come in. The symbolic message, here, is to remember consciously. Lord Shiva is symbolic of awakened consciousness. He crushes unmindful memory under His foot. Kashmiri Shaivism talks about recognizing—to *re-cognize*.'

Lopamudra: '*Pratyabhijna.*'

Dharma Raj: 'Yes. Don't re-live, remember—with wisdom. With cognition. Take charge.'

Lopamudra smiled. 'The Chidambaram Nataraja is called *Sabayil Aadum Eesan,* or "Sabesan" in short— the God who dances in the hall of consciousness. The Nataraja is you, can be you, dancing in the hall of consciousness after conquering Apasmara. "Apa" is to "lose" or "leave"; "smara" is "memory". In short, lose the memory that drags you down.'

Dharma Raj: 'We may be unwilling to change.'

Lopamudra: 'That's right. But if we are willing, not just to tinker and change some elements in ourselves, but to transform, then Apasmara is the essence of the process. It takes us from the psychological infancy of being buffeted by triggered emotions from the memory library, to becoming a mindful human being. Conquering Apasmara translates intention into practise.'

Dharma Raj: 'Lord Shiva's ultimate message is to not judge yourself. If you judge, you will not know your whole truth. See the bad boy and bad girl inside you. Take charge. But like a parent, you must do this with joy, ease, and kindness towards the "child".'

Lopamudra: 'And, the last pose in the Tandava dance is the Moksha Tandava. It expresses blissful freedom.'

Gargi: 'Wouldn't chasing blissful freedom take you back to the ego?'

Lopamudra: 'The ego does not know what true bliss is. It mistakes other things for bliss.'

Gargi: 'Like?'

Lopamudra: 'Like excitement. Passion. Achievement. Appreciation. Praise. Also, feeling superior, powerful, victorious, exulting. Basically, the ego thinks self-exaggeration is bliss.'

Nachiket: 'Also, I would think that if there's chasing involved, the goal cannot be bliss.'

Dharma Raj: 'Bliss is found in responsibility, effort, awareness, and a flip in "forgetfulness". Apasmara flips in the Moksha Tandava pose. In all the other poses of the Tandava dance, Apasmara lies on his stomach with his face turned away from Lord Shiva, whose foot is firmly planted on Apasmara's back. In the Moksha Tandava, Lord Shiva has flipped and His feet point upwards, while He rests His left hand on Apasmara's torso. Apasmara lies on his back. Both are looking into each other's eyes.'[85]

Gargi: '*Har Har Mahadev!*'

Nachiket: 'Can our *Ishta Devata* change at this stage, with our awakening consciousness? Can we begin to be pulled by another God or Goddess?'

Dharma Raj: 'Yes. But it's more likely that the pantheon expands while Lord Shiva does not loosen His hold. We may start getting attracted to others *also*. Transformation and an awakened consciousness can open our hearts to abundance and steadiness.'

Lopamudra: 'Abundance and steadiness. Like Goddesses Laxmi and Saraswati?'

Dharma Raj smiled.

12

POWER OF THE GODDESS

The pizza delivery boy opened the gate just as Gargi poured the last of the wine into Anirban's glass. They had enjoyed it so much that they had opened another bottle. Nachiket walked up and took the boxes from the delivery boy Gargi changed the music to a Yaman medley of Bollywood songs.

Gargi: 'I present to you—a Madhuraa Bhattacharya Yaman medley! *Haay mar jaayenge ... haay lut jaayenge ... aisi baaten kiya na karo ...*'

Nachiket: '... *Aaj jaane ki zid na karo* ... I love you, Mrs Sawant.'

Gargi: 'Under strict terms and conditions, Mr Sawant.'

Nachiket laughed.

Lopamudra Mondal Deshpande got up and moved indoors, a faint smile hovering on her face. Dr Adarsh's phone began to ring. He grabbed it and moved away from the others.

Nachiket placed the pizzas on the dining table and returned outside.

The next song began ...

'Jab deep jale aana ... jab sham dhale aana ...'

The group began to sing along.

And the next …

'*Ehsaan tera hoga mujhpar …*'

Lopamudra walked out with a bowl of gulab jamuns on a tray. She sat in the chair next to her husband.

'*Is mod se jaate hain …*'

'*Chandan sa badan, chanchal chitwan …*' Dharma Raj reached for his wife's hand.

The next …

'*Beeti na bitaaye raina …*'

'*Paan khaye saiyaan hamaaro …*'

Gargi got up from her seat, sashayed outside the circle of chairs, and swirled around with her arms stretched wide and her face thrown back. She swayed her hips and laughed aloud. Nachiket laughed delightedly and joined her.

Lopamudra: 'Gargi is a Yaman girl.'

Anirban: 'Well, I've just discovered that I'm a Yaman boy. These are my favourite songs. All inspired by Raga Yaman.'

Dr Adarsh walked back and took a chair.

Lopamudra: '*Shaub kichu theek acche? (Everything all right?)*'

Dr Adarsh: 'Yes. That was Shirish. I spoke to him after almost a month. He's been hiking in the Andes.'

Anirban: 'Did he go to Machu Picchu?'

Dr Adarsh: 'Yes, he did the Inca trail.'

Lopamudra: 'You know what I would really like to do? The Ramayana trail in Sri Lanka. I believe it's special.'

Dharma Raj picked up a cheese-laden pizza slice.

Dharma Raj: 'Maybe we can do it together. Rameshwaram and then Sri Lanka.'

Anirban: 'I'd love that. I will arrange it. I think Malivalaya might join us for this one. Sometime in December?'

Nachiket: 'Let's see. Gargi, can we listen to Mohammed Rafi now? Only till we finish the meal.'

Gargi: 'Okay. Papa will like that too.

'*Likhe jo khat tujhe ... wo teri yaad mein ...*'

The Goddess could wait—music, Her creation, was captivating enough.

'Abundance. Fullness. That's Goddess Laxmi,' Dharma Raj murmured, almost inaudibly.

Anirban: 'Abundance as in wealth, right?'

Dharma Raj: 'Not quite. Shri Laxmi's association with wealth is a sign of the reductionist times we live in.'[86]

Lopamudra: 'Reductionist and materialistic.'

Nachiket: 'I don't know where this is going, but it's true that happiness is defined by achievements and possessions today. Self-love trumps self-analysis.'

Anirban: 'And displaying self-confidence beats being self-restrained.'

Dr Adarsh: 'Uncle, you really turn our common understanding upside down. Tell us about Goddess Laxmi. You called her Shri Laxmi.'

Rishi Durvasa is given to frequent anger. He curses Lord Indra and, resultantly, the Lord of the Gods loses Indralok, his beloved kingdom, to the great Asura king, Bali. Distraught, Lord Indra approaches Lord Vishnu for help. Lord Vishnu advises that the Gods and Asuras perform the Samudra Manthan[87]—the churning of the Ocean—on Anant Chaturdashi and settle the matter. Mount Mandar serves as the dasher and Vasuki, king of the serpents, wraps himself around the mountain and becomes the rope around the dasher. Lord Vishnu transforms Himself into Kurma, the tortoise, and lodges Himself underneath the great mountain as the stabilizing base.

The first churning brings forth *halahal*, the terrible *blue poison of chaos and destruction*. Lord Shiva, compassionate and detached, swallows the poison and lodges it in His throat, which turns blue and luminescent.

The churning resumes. Navratnas, the nine precious gems emerge. Chandra, the moon emerges. The Parijata tree, with the delicate, fragrant white flowers with an orange stem emerges. Then comes Kamadhenu, the sacred, plentiful mother cow. Then follows Airavata, the magnificent four-tusked white elephant who serves as the mount of Lord Indra, the king of the Gods.

Madira, the Goddess of Wine, is brought forth. She marries Lord Varuna, Lord of the Waters, and thereafter is also known as Varuni. Kalpavriksha, the wish-fulfilling tree appears. Next, the Apsaras—water nymphs—who are also the celestial dancers. Ucchaishravas, the seven-headed celestial horse, surfaces. Panchajanya, the conch of Lord Vishnu, comes to form. Then, Sharanga, the magic bow of Lord Vishnu. Also, Kaumodaki, Lord Vishnu's mace. The Kaustubha gem appears. Dhanvantari, the physician of the Gods, arrives with *amrita* (*nectar*), the drink of immortality.

And, of course, the resplendent Shri Laxmi, Goddess of abundance and bounty. She desires Lord Vishnu, the Sustainer, Who accepts Her as His consort.

Goddess Laxmi is worshipped during Diwali, the festival of Lights. It's interesting that on this occasion, She is accompanied by Lord Ganesh in the ritual ceremony, and not Lord Vishnu, Her husband. Nor Lord Shiva or Goddess Parvati, Lord Ganesh's parents. Or Lord Kartikeya, His brother.

Lord Ganesh symbolizes wisdom. He can transform the 'obstacles' of life into 'opportunities'. This transformation then leads to the true meaning of Goddess Laxmi: abundant fulfilment and defeat of darkness.

Popular iconography depicts Her resplendently dressed, seated on a lotus. She holds a lotus in each of Her upper hands, and the *jyoti kalash—the proverbial pot of light*—in another hand. Sometimes. At other times, that hand is in the *varada mudra*, granting abundance. Wealth pours out of Her fourth hand in the form of gold coins.

Goddess Laxmi has other names: Padmaa, Padmaja, Kamalaa, Shubhaa, Ramaa, Sujata, Narayani, Vishnupriya and Haripriya. She is also Ashta Laxmi, the one with eight manifestations: Adi Lakshmi, Dhanya Lakshmi, Dhairya Lakshmi, Gaja Lakshmi, Santaana Lakshmi, Vijaya Lakshmi, Vidya Lakshmi and Dhana Lakshmi.

What happens after Goddess Laxmi emerges from the milky white ocean that is churned? Dhanvantari, physician to the Gods, emerges from the froth and foam of the churn. He holds a pot in one hand and the Ayur Veda in his other hand. The pot contains *amrit* (*the elixir of immortality*).

All that has emerged until then has been shared between the Devas and Asuras. But the elixir creates a problem. The Gods and Asuras begin to quarrel over it. Lord Vishnu now takes the form of Mohini, the enchantress, and ensures that immortality is for the Gods.

Dharma Raj: 'Goddess Laxmi's teachings have largely been appropriated by today's materialism, Adarsh. "Shri" is "radiance". Shri Laxmi is the Goddess of Radiance and Abundance. But what do you think abundance is?'

Dr Adarsh: 'It cannot only mean brands, gadgets and stuff!'

Gargi: 'More's the pity! Papa, you said fullness, and full is the opposite of empty. Then an exuberant heart is Goddess Laxmi. A fearless heart is Goddess Laxmi.'

Nachiket: 'Fear empties your heart, that's true.'

Anirban: 'What if I think I'm already fearless? And what do we fear, anyway?'

Gargi: 'If you think you're fearless then you need to think some more!'

Anirban raised his brows.

Lopamudra: 'We fear many things: Betrayal. Hurt. Abandonment. Loss of face. Being insulted. Being ignored. Loss, just loss. Sometimes these fears have good reasons. Sometimes they don't. Often, they're rooted in a past event that's long gone. But the emotion and its memory persist.'

Dr Adarsh: 'You are saying that fear will limit abundance. How?'

Gargi: 'Fear makes you miserly in expressing love, for instance. You fear rejection. Or it can make you express too much love. You fake it or overdo it. Fear makes you judgemental and watchful. Or suspicious. You develop serious trust issues. You keep testing people's love for you. You're either scared to give, or you give too much in relationships and get depleted.'

Anirban: 'Get depleted of what?'

Gargi: 'Energy. Sustained energy. A fearful heart also limits your ability to receive love. You're scared of losing it, so you hold too tight.'

Nachiket: 'But genuine love has got to be selfless. Or else it's not love.'

Dr Adarsh: 'It can be, actually. It's self-love.'

Lopamudra: 'Which often is not love. Love must expand our hearts. Love, abundant love, is respectful *towards everything and everyone*. No exclusivity. An abundant, love-filled heart experiences life to the fullest.'

Gargi: 'But isn't love interpersonal? Isn't it something that two people share?'

Dharma Raj: 'That is not the love we're talking about right now. That kind of love is Lord Krishna-like. It is important, with its beauty and heartaches, but it is different. Goddess Laxmi's love is not found in relationships. Her love is abundance and fullness. It's the radiating power of positive energy. It is the absence of void. Opposite of emptiness, as you said, Gargi.'

Lopamudra: 'Positive energy radiates when the heart is full.'

Gargi: 'So, Goddess Laxmi attracts those who are in need of abundance. Maybe because they are empty. That's why She holds the *jyoti kalash*.'

Lopamudra: 'And wealth pours out of another hand. It is pouring *out*. If you want to experience abundance, be generous. Riches are not for grabbing but giving.'

Dr Adarsh: 'I don't know why, but I just thought of Shirish's description of his affluent friends from California. All of them have a personal life expert.'

Gargi: 'What's that?'

Dr Adarsh: 'Someone who helps you deal with life. Who helps you understand why your life feels so empty, despite having it all, doing it all, seeing it all.'

Gargi: 'No abundance in your heart but you're surrounded by plenty. Just chasing excitement all the time. Like a drug addict chasing the next fix. All you will get is momentary pleasure, followed by even more emptiness and sadness.'

Nachiket: 'Exactly. The problem with excitement is that there is a peak and then a dip. Then you start looking for the next high.'

Lopamudra: 'Abundance has nothing to do with thrills and things. Goddess Laxmi is stifled when you hoard Her or waste Her. She flees and leaves emptiness behind.'

Nachiket: 'Gratitude creates an abundant heart.'

Gargi: 'Actually, real fullness lies in a love-filled heart. And a joy-filled heart. No matter what the circumstances. Gratitude is very nice. But Goddess Laxmi is just a love-filled heart.'

Anirban: 'Also a fearless heart?'

Lopamudra: 'They're tied together. Abundance leaves no place for fear. And love and joy know no fear.'

Dr Adarsh: 'What about the misery of love? The agony and the ecstasy, like the songs and poems tell us.'

Gargi: 'That's human drama, Adarsh. Self-indulgent theatre. Self-love. If love makes you sad then it is not real love, because then it is self-absorbed and insecure. In any case, it is not Goddess Laxmi-love. Ma, that's the messaging of Her lotuses, isn't it?'

Lopamudra: 'You're right, *mulgi majhi* (*my child*). The beautiful lotus grows in a dirty pond. Regardless of circumstance, you can bloom. Look around you carefully. Joy is not an external arrangement.'

Anirban: 'Malivalaya told me a Zen proverb the other day, "Before enlightenment one chops wood and carries water. After enlightenment one chops wood and carries water."[88] Couldn't make sense of it then.'

Dharma Raj: 'Says it all. External life may remain the same, or it may transform. It doesn't matter. Radiance changes the life within. Whatever you do, you do it with beauty. You live in grace.'

Gargi: 'Like Shakkubai. *Sadaa sukhi* (*forever happy*).'

Dr Adarsh: 'Who's Shakkubai?'

Lopamudra: 'My house-help. She has an alcoholic husband. Five children. A useless brother and an old mother, whom she supports … Recently her home was brought down by the Pune Municipal Corporation. Raj helped her rebuild it.'

Nachiket: 'But she's the happiest person I know. Barring, of course, my Gargi!'

Anirban: 'So, Shakkubai is a true devotee of Goddess Laxmi?!'

Gargi: 'Absolutely!'

Nachiket: 'Everyone has problems. What counts is what we make of them and what we make of ourselves.'

Anirban: 'If you allow me a slight detour here, I have one question. What about poor King Bali? Lord Indra lost his Indralok to him. So what? Wasn't Bali a great king? Why is he demonized in North India?'

Lopamudra: 'Who told you that he is demonized in North India? Western Missionary propaganda has pulled out this narrative from its agenda-driven hat and made Bali a great "Dravidian" leader undone by a North Indian nefarious God. I'll have you know that this great "Dravidian" leader is celebrated and revered by Hindus, including so-called "Aryan" Northies. This is just like the newfound belief from some Marxist handbooks of Hinduism that Raavan is a "Dravidian" leader who was defeated by a "North Indian" upper-caste God. When, actually, Raavan was a Brahmin born close to Delhi, in a place called Bisrakh. One of the oldest temples dedicated to Raavan is in Bisrakh, by the way ...'

Dharma Raj: 'Lopa, Lopa, Lopa ... Let's keep politics out, madam ji.'

Anirban: 'Uncle! Uncle! Uncle! Just this once, please. This sounds very interesting to me. Please note, I'm a

South Indian sitting amidst a bevy of Northies. And I'm
married to a half-Sikhni!'

Lopamudra: 'This is Maharashtra, Anirban. It is
neither north nor south; it is west!'

Everyone laughed softly.

'In any case,' continued Lopamudra, 'Anirban, during
the festival of Rakhi, a sister is supposed to recite a
mantra while tying the thread around her brother's wrist.
Raj, recite the mantra.'

Dharma Raj: 'Okay...

Yena baddho Bali raja,
Daanavendro mahaabalah
Tena tvaam abhibaddhnaami
Rakshe maachal maachalah

I tie this thread of protection,
The same that had bound king Bali, the Mighty,
the Charitable,
O thread of protection, be stable, be firm.'[89]

Lopamudra: 'This mantra is recited not just on rakhi,
once a year, but every time a *puja* ends and the *kalaava*
(*sacred thread*) is tied on the wrist by the priest.'

The great King Bali, Lord of the Asuras, organizes the
ritual sacrifice for Lord Vishnu the Sustainer. Lord
Vishnu decides to put this great devotee to the test. So,
He appears in the midst of the ritual as Vaaman, the

diminutive boy-priest and asks the king for only three footsteps of Mother Earth. The great king readily nods in agreement. Bewilderingly, the boy-priest grows in size and soon straddles all of creation. He takes his first step; it covers *Bhoomidevi* (*Mother Earth*). With his second step he covers the sky. He looks down at his devotee with feigned befuddlement. Now what?

King Bali becomes aware of his Lord's intentions. He recognizes his true Lord in the now-not-diminutive boy-priest. He comes near His feet and bows his head with grand humility. The noble king offers his head as the ground for the third step. Pleased, Lord Vishnu asks that he becomes the Lord of Sutala Loka, the third realm of Patala, the netherworld.

From this day onwards, Lord Vishnu is Trivikram, the Lord of the Three Strides. The one who beholds the humility in King Bali, the Lord of the Underworld.

Having sacrificed his all to the Lord, King Bali asks Lord Vishnu to accompany him to the netherworld that he has been pushed into. Lord Vishnu is compelled to respond to this exemplary devotee who has passed His test of character with flying colours. He abandons Vaikunth, His abode, and accompanies Bali to Sutala Loka.

Meanwhile, Goddess Laxmi finds Herself alone in Vaikunth. The Goddess of Abundance experiences the pangs of abandonment. She wants Her consort back home. She changes form and approaches King Bali as a poor, decrepit woman. King Bali kindly offers Her shelter in his home and a place in his heart as his sister.

On full moon night in the month of Shravan, Goddess Laxmi, still in the form of the poor woman, approaches Her brother King Bali and ties a thread of protection around the wrist of his right hand. The gracious king offers his sister a gift She desires, along with his lifelong protection. Goddess Laxmi now transfigures into Her resplendent form and asks for the return of Lord Vishnu, Her husband. True to his word, the great king sets Lord Vishnu free.

Before leaving the netherworld, Lord Vishnu makes a commitment to His noble devotee—heretofore He will spend four months in a year with King Bali in the netherworld. It is the period of *chaturmaas*, which commences on Devshayani Ekadashi—the eleventh day of Shukla Paksha, the bright fortnight—in the month of Ashadha. It ends on Devotthan Ekadashi—the eleventh day of the bright fortnight in the month of Kartik. The latter is the day Lord Vishnu awakens from *chaturmaas*, His four months of penance and *tapa*.

The Lord also promises that at the end of Kali yuga, King Mahabali will be the next Indra and will reside in Indra loka.

King Bali, also known as Maveli and Indrasenan, is the grandson of Bhakt Prahlad, the grand icon among devotees. He is Chiranjeevi, the Immortal.[90]

Lopamudra: 'Coming back to Goddess Laxmi, She has another steady companion besides Lord Ganesh—Goddess Saraswati. Raj says that without Her, Goddess Laxmi's fullness is *chanchal* (*flickering*).'

Anirban: 'Why will a full and abundant heart feel empty without Goddess Saraswati? She is art, right?'

Dharma Raj: 'Saying that Goddess Saraswati is art is like calling the Bhagavad Gita a book. It is much more.'

Gargi: 'Much, much, much more!'

Lopamudra: 'For once, your overstatement is not sounding over the top, Gargi!'

Lord Brahma wakes up from sleep and creates the cosmic universe. Alas, it is gooey and has no order or form. He needs the assistance of Embodied Knowledge. The Creator must first make Creativity.

Lord Brahma conceives this Embodiment of Knowledge from His mind. She emerges, pristine and pure. He names Her Saraswati and She helps Him create the forms: the Sun, the Moon, the stars, the planets, the oceans ...

Lord Brahma is mesmerized by all that they create. He is spellbound by Her, the gorgeous personification of all accomplishment—Goddess Saraswati. He pins His eyes on Her. She circumambulates in reverence. He grows a head in each direction, so that He can gaze at Her moving. Five heads, with one atop His central head—to see Her.

The Goddess transforms into a doe and escapes into the skies. Lord Brahma quickly takes the form of an antelope and rushes after Her, hypnotized. Rudra the Archer[91] brings the frantic pursuit to a swift end by lopping off Lord Brahma's extra heads.[92] Clear-headed now, the Lord of Creation seeks to break out of the grip of desire. Serene Goddess Saraswati reveals to Him the secret of unshackling and liberation.

Creativity has form and is stable now, and Lord Brahma decides to conduct the great ritual yagna. He needs a consort for the ceremony and Goddess Saraswati quietly seats Herself to His left.[93] It is a union of the God of Creation and the Goddess of Knowledge and its offshoots: speech, music, art and language.

Her names echo Her symbology: Vaagdevi, Vaani, Bhaarati, Vaagishwari … She is also known as Sharada, Shataroopa and Veenakaraa.

She is usually seated on a white lotus beside a flowing river, dressed in pristine white. The waters subtly allude to Her connection with River Saraswati. She holds the Vedas in Her left lower hand, and the prayer beads in the right upper hand. The other two hands strum the Veena. Sometimes She holds a pot of water in one of Her hands.

The Vedas represent knowledge, and the prayer beads, reflection. The Veena is harmonious music. Harmony. In some distant future, when our speech, thought, emotion, and behaviour are in sync, then our life will flow like the melodious sound of Goddess Saraswati's Veena.

Sometimes She rides a white *hamsa*. At other times, the *swan* loiters at Her feet. The colour white symbolizes the Satvika light of knowledge, and the swan represents the ability to discern. The *hamsa* mythically separates milk from water.

Sometimes a peacock preens in the vicinity; the ultimate symbol of beauty.

She was born on the fifth day of the month of Magha, in Shukla Paksha or the fortnight of the waxing moon. Hindus celebrate the day as Basant Panchami. It heralds the spring and, on this day, She is worshipped in homes, schools and all institutes of art and learning.

Dharma Raj: 'When your heart is full, you're a secure person. But insecurity can be a terrible thing. It never gives up and creeps up on you when you least expect it. It haunts the most compassionate and strong people. Positivity is not easy to hold on to, and you falter every now and then. Goddess Laxmi's friend, Goddess Saraswati, makes you steady. She stops the faltering.'

Dr Adarsh: 'Chalam had called Goddess Saraswati the counterpart of Goddess Laxmi. Interesting.'[94]

Anirban: 'I still don't see the connection completely, but please go on. Sorry for interrupting.'

Gargi: '*Aadat se majboor! (Constrained by habit!)*'

Anirban: 'Look who's talking!'

Dharma Raj continued, 'Goddess Saraswati is actually our distilled essence. She's our best self, the ultimate personification of intelligence, intuition, beauty, balance, stillness and wisdom.'

Lopamudra: 'And wisdom is beyond knowledge. Today people think that knowledge and reason are the ultimate.'

Anirban: 'Reason and logic are important. Precious.'

Lopamudra: 'Oh yes, they are. No doubt. I'm not devaluing them. Reason and logic are useful. But wisdom has reason and something more. Intuition. Reason and intuition must be a marriage of equals ... Goddess Saraswati requires persistence, reflection. Hard work.'

Nachiket: 'Her popular understanding is knowledge, music, dance, poetry, literature ...'

Dharma Raj: 'Those are the means through which we meet Her. *Maybe*. But She is much more than all this. She takes your *in*-stretched hand when you're ready for the inward journey.'

Lopamudra: 'In a state of aloneness?'

Dharma Raj: 'In a state of aloneness. Not loneliness, mind you.'

Dr Adarsh: 'Reminds me of a beautiful phrase used by Manoj Chalam: a "duet of one". Although he used it when he spoke about Lord Shiva.'[95]

Gargi: 'Nice. Very apt for the Goddess as well. And since the evening has been so much about music, do you think we can talk about *muraliwala* (*the flute player*)?'

Nachiket: 'Lord Krishna!'

13

THE DARK-SKINNED LORD

'K*atha*' is a 'story', and 'Kathak' is 'storytelling'. Kathak is also a classical Indian dance form and Lopamudra had introduced Gargi to it when she was five. Kathak, in turn, introduced Gargi to her *Ishta Devata*: Lord Krishna the Cowherd. Her *didima (maternal grandmother)* gifted her a brass idol of Lord Bal Gopal when she was ten. Ever since, Gargi performed a private ritual for Lord Krishna, the child, every morning; it was her *puja*.

Gargi loved Lord Krishna. And Gargi was all heart. Volatile, prickly, opinionated, and wilfull, yes, but all heart. No malice. No hidden agenda.

Dharma Raj: 'Lord Krishna is love. Joy. Pain. Joy. Duets … Multiple duets … Joy!'

Nachiket: 'Meaning?'

A child is born to Devaki and Vasudev on a dark, stormy night of Krishna Paksha Ashtami—the eighth night of the waning moon—in the rainy month of Shravan. He gurgles with delight. He does not cry. His parents languish in jail.

Kansa, His uncle, has sworn to kill all their children as it has been foretold that their eighth child will kill him. Little Krishna is the eighth child.

His father, Vasudev, snuggles the silent baby in a wicker basket and smuggles Him out of Mathura in the middle of the night.

Vasudev steps into a raging River Yamuna, headed towards Gokul on the other side. The river rises ferociously and almost trips the spindly, shaky man with a wicker basket balanced on his head. The river only craves to touch the child's feet, Little Krishna knows, so He sticks out a foot. Yamuna calms down immediately. Vasuki, the king of serpents, rises from the depths and raises his hood over the basket, protecting the Lord on this rain-drenched night.

Gokul, the village of cowherds, is sound asleep. Vasudev enters the home of Nanda, the chief of the village, and finds his wife, Yashoda, asleep after giving birth to a baby girl. He exchanges the babies with Nanda's help and leaves, bereft. The baby girl—Goddess Yogmaya—later survives Kansa's attack.

Yashoda names Him 'Shyam', the dark-skinned one. She adores Him. The village adores Him. He is the beloved of the cowherds and the milkmaids. But the infant is in danger. Kansa learns that Devaki's eighth child has survived and sends Putana, the demoness, who fills her breasts with poisoned milk to kill Shyam. He sucks the life out of her. Kansa then sends Shakata, the demon, who hides within the spokes of a cartwheel and hurtles towards the baby. Shyam kicks it to smithereens. Nanda and Yashoda begin to fear for the life of their precious baby and move to Vrindavana, an idyllic patch of land at the foot of Govardhan mountain on the banks of River Yamuna. It is dotted with the auspicious *tulsi* (*basil plant*). The entire village migrates with them. Why would anyone live without their favourite toddler?

The dangers persist in Vrindavana. Kaaliya, the many-hooded serpent attacks Shyam as He bathes in the Yamuna. He subdues the snake with ease and dances on his hoods, even as the wind, river, trees and birds make music. Shyam's rhythmic heartbeats provide the *taal*.

Yashoda dresses Him like a girl.[96] Maybe it will keep Him safe? The child absorbs the feminine impulse … He learns that He can delight. He learns that He can sadden. He notices that His emotional state is mirrored in others around Him. If He is upset, they are sad. If He is happy, they are delighted. If He makes himself vulnerable, it brings out the protective impulse. He takes control and begins to guide emotions. The master human handler begins His *leela* (*the enactment of the colours of emotion*).

At dawn, He accompanies the cowherds to the slopes of Govardhan and plays the flute. The cows graze better. They give more milk. Later He teases the milkmaids and steals their butter, even their garments. He beguiles them with His flute and delights them with His antics. He chases them and breaks their pots of water. He is the beloved prankster. He is the beloved. As He chucks a pebble, He looks at a milkmaid. She is noticed; seen fully, attentively. For that moment, she is special. He has driven away the loneliness one feels with distracted attention. If He does not turn up to drench them with water, they are lonely. Alone. For Shyam knows the art of paying full attention to another.

Lord Indra lets loose the Madhuvana forests the stormy clouds one day. It is as if Vrindavana will drown. Lord Krishna leads them all to Govardhan and raises the mountain aloft on His little finger. Perfectly balanced. All are sheltered. All are safe.

He is the beautiful, dark-skinned God who wears yellow clothes and a peacock feather on His crown. He has curly hair, graceful limbs and a naughty smile playing on His face.

Krishna. Shyam. Gopal. Giridhar. Nandalal. Yashodanandan. Devakinandan. Sakha. Saarthi. Manmohan.

He protects. He loves. He nurtures. He is masculine. He is feminine. He is complete.

Lopamudra: 'Lord Krishna is the template for every flavour and form of love in relationships. He is both *makhan chor* and *chit chor*—He *steals butter* and *He steals hearts*. He is *tribhanga* (*bent in three places*) while He plays the flute. How does one remove the twisting one—the one who is not straight—from the heart?! He loves them all. They fall in love with Him, for He falls in love with them.'

Dharma Raj: 'On moonlit nights He plays the flute in the Madhuvana forests on the riverbank. The gopis gather around Him and dance in circles all night. It is the *Raas mandala* (*the cosmic dance of love*). Lord Krishna plays the flute in the centre and also dances with each of them, simultaneously. In a duet with all.'

Lopamudra: 'Some say to themselves, "Shyam is mine. And mine alone." They are broken and hurt by life. They crave exclusivity and the repeated message that they matter. They take …

'And then one says to the others, "Shyam is mine. And yours too." She is Radha. The unbroken one. She knows inclusivity. She gives. She receives …'

Nachiket: 'Some want and are dissatisfied. Others have and are satisfied … Lord Krishna brings emotions to the surface and makes them recognizable. This is crucial, for only then can emotions be transformed. It's a movement from wanting to having, craving to being, possessing to freeing …'

Gargi: 'From wanting to please to being content?'

Lopamudra: 'Yes. But Lord Krishna is needed within us for this. He is patient, love is patient. To love is to see. To see more. To show. To show more. To listen. To hear. To feel. To feel more … To protect. To give solace. To beguile. To unbeguile. To guide. To confuse. To test. To challenge. To bind. To let go. To give. To receive. To hurt. To delight. To attach. To detach. To enable bliss.'

Dharma Raj laughs softly. He looks at his wife, a glance that no one notices. Except one. Nachiket.

Dharma Raj: 'But the fixed ingredient is regard. If you don't have regard for a person, then you don't really love that person.'

Gargi: 'Name some types of love.'

Dharma Raj: 'Number one is mother's love, unconditional and nurturing. Like Ma Yashoda's love for Shyam.'

Lopamudra: 'Gargi, you said that Nachiket's love has terms and conditions; it is not unconditional.'

Gargi: 'It isn't.'

Lopamudra: 'And, you would like to be loved unconditionally.'

'Don't we all?' Gargi threw the words with deep emotion.

Lopamudra: 'Do you love him unconditionally?'

Gargi's voice was strangled. 'I try to.'

Dharma Raj gently took over from his wife. 'To love is a constant state of being. When you love someone, it doesn't decrease or increase, at different times and in different situations. You just love. That's it. *Expression* of love is different. It is a softness in our conduct towards the loved one. And that must be conditional, always and for all. And it begins with me. The first person who must receive conditional expression of love is me. Earn it. Earn the softness in conduct from those around you.'

Lopamudra: 'But infants are an exception. They must know unconditional, soft love from their mothers. Like Lord Bal Gopal and Ma Yashoda.'

Dharma Raj: 'Yes. That is crucial. Lord Krishna-love from the mother, which is attentive, creates Goddess Laxmi-like fullness of the heart and self-assurance in an infant; an abundant heart. It guarantees future security and joy. No emptiness. In all other cases, we must earn the expression of love. It must begin with "me", "my" conduct. Give freely. Earn the receiving.'

Gargi: 'I'll think about this.'

Anirban: 'I suggest you do the thinking tomorrow. Like Scarlett O'Hara in *Gone with the Wind*.'

Gargi scowled at him. Then broke into a smile.

Lopamudra squeezed her daughter's hand and moved the conversation forward. 'There are other forms of Lord Krishna-love. It can be passionate and playful and steeped in musical sensuality, like with Goddess Radha.'

Nachiket glanced at his wife. No one noticed. She did and smiled.

Dharma Raj: 'Sometimes it is a mature and respectful companionship, like His enduring relationship with Goddess Rukmini. Alone. Together.'

Nachiket: 'Like your relationship, Ma and Papa.'

Dharma Raj: 'It still has its playful moments, you know!'

'Only in his imagination,' Lopamudra teased.

Nachiket: 'Goddess Rukmini stands alone even in Pandharpur, not just in Dwaraka. There is Her temple and then there is the Vitthal temple. Gargi, a poem for Goddess Rukmini? You'd read some Marathi poems to me once, I remember.'

Gargi: 'Okay ... I will choose a few lines to convey this flavour ... This is a poem by Sneha Datar,[97] a very sensitive poetess:

> *Vaam bhaag tu aslees zari ti*
> *Poorna aahe to phakta tujhyaat*
> *... Garajach naahi maj bhaase tya*
> *Bhetichi mug Vittoos aaj ...*

Translate, my good man?'

Nachiket closed his eyes,

> *'Perched to His left, had You been,*
> *Complete He still would be, within You.*
> *...Where then be, another need?*
> *Why seek Him at all?'*

Mischievous Sage Narada offers a single Parijat flower to Lord Krishna while He is in the company of His intellectual companion, Goddess Rukmini. Lord Krishna takes it in His right hand and presents it to His graceful consort. She accepts the flower with adoration and love. She observes with delight that its delicate white petals are held together by a startling orange stem. She is happy.

Sage Narada now leaves the couple and makes his way next door to Satyabhama, Lord Krishna's warrior-wife, and describes the fragile flower to her in detail. She is mesmerized. She wants one. He then slyly throws in the small detail—Lord Krishna has just gifted the flower to Goddess Rukmini. Satyabhama is seized by snake-like tentacles of anger and jealousy. She leaves her abode in fury and barges into the courtyard, and then the household of Goddess Rukmini. She heads straight for the couple seated in the Garden of Goddess Rukmini and demands that her husband give her not just the single flower, but the entire Parijat tree.

Lord Krishna must placate His combatant wife, but the divine Parijat tree is planted in Amravati, the realm of Lord Indra, king of the Gods. Lord Krishna leaves for Amravati, accompanied by His warrior-wife Satyabhama. On reaching the abode of Lord Indra, Lord Krishna uproots the tree, and after facing daunting travails in the realm they make their way back home.

Satyabhama has her Parijat tree. But who escapes the entrapment of consequences? Satyabhama's jealousy and anger have repercussions, as do Goddess Rukmini's grace and large-heartedness. Lord Krishna plants the Parijat tree in Satyabhama's Garden, but it abuts the border between the palaces of His two wives. The irony dawns upon Satyabhama when the tree is in bloom, for the celestial orange-stemmed flowers fall in the Garden of Goddess Rukmini.[98]

Interesting titbit: the Parijat flower is also called Shefali, a popular Indian name for girls.

Lopamudra: 'Meera's is the love of singular devotion. Goddess Radha's is the love of inclusion. Goddess Rukmini's is the love of completion. I am complete. You are complete. Together, we make a larger completion. A larger whole.'

Nachiket: '*Purnamadah purnamidam*
Purnaatpurnamudachyate
Purnasya purnamaadaaya
Purnamevaavashishyate.'

Dharma Raj: '*That is full. This is full.*
From the full comes the full.

Remove the full from the full
And what remains?
The full.'[99]

Dr Adarsh: 'Lord Krishna exhibits so many kinds of love. For instance, love for a friend. Like Udhava and Sudama.'

Lopamudra: 'Hmmm ... He sends Udhava to lovelorn Vrindavana to tell them that Shyam will never return. What must be done must be done. But never ignore an aching heart. It is a central lesson from Lord Krishna—never ignore an aching heart.'

Shyam must leave Vrindavana, never to return. This slice of life is over. Yashoda. Radha. Cowherds. Milkmaids. The flute. The playfulness, the *raas leela* ... Life starts afresh with new relationships. He reaches Mathura and fulfils His destiny by killing His cruel uncle Kansa. The cowherd is now a warrior. Bhakti yoga is over. It is time for karma yoga. And karma yoga needs training.

Lord Krishna goes to Rishi Sandipani's ashram for education. The cowherd learns refinement, statecraft, warrior craft, philosophy, aesthetics, logic. He returns to Mathura where the world of politics awaits Him. But bereft Vrindavana needs a final emotional stroke.

He sends His gurukul friend, Udhava, to Vrindavana to tell the people that He will not return. Udhava reaches lovelorn Vrindavana. He appeals to their *manas* (*mind*). He tells them suffering is illusion. Separation is illusion. He asks them to shed *bhoga* (*enjoyment*) and elevate *bhava* (*emotion*). He exhorts them to move to the centre. From longing to equanimity.

Vrindavana responds. Radha responds. They teach Him that emotions matter. It is the *raas leela*. Even *maya* (*illusion*), has purpose. Udhava's understanding is deepened.

Years later, during the great solar eclipse, the kings and commoners gather at the Samantapanchaka for a ritual bath. The wives of Lord Krishna conspire one morning to visit the cowherd community of Vraja which has camped on the other side of the five lakes. They wish to see Radha. Was she beautiful? Was she radiant? What was she like, this beloved of their Lord Krishna?

The regal queens of Dwaraka wade across to the other side and wend their way among the mass of cowherds and milkmaids, bonny girls and boisterous boys, industrious old women and gossiping old men! They find her, a simple milkmaid. Radha. She is ordinary, everyday. Her skin is weathered by age and the sun. Fine lines fan out from the sides of her eyes and ends of her lips. She is making cow dung cakes. And singing. She looks up, startled, as the bevy of fine ladies approach her with curiosity writ large across their beautiful faces. She meets them with enthusiasm and offers them some butter; her Shyam's favourite.[100]

Radha understood that her Lord Krishna loved them all. Loved it all. No butter, no milk, no milkmaid, no cowherd, no queen, no friend was really His *only* special one.

Gokul. Vrindavana. Mathura. Dwaraka ... Lord Krishna does not return. He only moves forward. There is no reconnection with the past. Love wraps itself within the folds of heartbreak. It also nestles within a large, inclusive heart.

Knowledge resides in the mind. It is incomplete. Love dwells in the heart. It completes.

Dharma Raj: 'Udhava tells the *Krishna-deewanas*—intoxicated with devotional love—to be equanimous. Life is an illusion. Move on.'

Lopamudra: 'But then Udhava himself is schooled in matters of the heart. A love-drenched Radha responds, "Why move on? Why move on from sweetness? Why move on when grief itself is ennobling? We have known unconditional love and beauty. We have bloomed. Why leave behind memories that elevate emotion to the sweetest sentiment? Why let go of a love that centres? That does not scatter? That elevates desire itself into an instrument of growth? We yearn. We endlessly yearn.

We suffer, but our suffering is sweet..." This is *bhakti* (*devotion*).'

Nachiket: 'And then, there is the other very interesting friend—Sudama.'

Lord Krishna meets Sudama in Rishi Sandipani's ashram and the two strike a deep bond of friendship. They part at the end of their education.

Years go by and one day Sudama visits Lord Krishna in Dwaraka unannounced. Lord Krishna receives His childhood friend as though expecting him that morning. He showers His love, affection, and attention on His long-lost friend. Lord Krishna asks for a gift! Sudama does not falter and offers Him *sattu*. Lord Krishna eats the humble gruel as if it is all He likes to eat.

The two friends enjoy each other's company and fondly recall the good times when they were young and carefree. Sudama has come to ask for help. He is much too poor and sustenance is difficult for him and his family. But he is embarrassed to ask so he returns without asking. He only gives ... And returns to material transformation. A plentiful home. His friend Lord Krishna's return gifts![101]

A true friend knows without being asked. He sees the need. He distinguishes the need from the greed.

Dr Adarsh: 'Lovely … Sudama brings sattu for Lord Krishna. My favourite.'

Gargi: 'It's pohe actually.'

Dr Adarsh: 'I think it's sattu.'

Lopamudra laughed. 'It is whatever Sudama offers. Don't you see? Whatever you give is exactly what Lord Krishna wants! He makes a thought arise in Sudama's mind: *Only me. Only I know what Lord Krishna wants! No one has fed Him sattu/pohe/makhane/whatever. No one can know! Only me! Lord Krishna's legion of number ones! You are special! You are seen! I witness you!*'

Gargi: 'Hmmm … Like when Lord Krishna visits Vidur's home in Hastinapur. Sulabha, Vidur's wife, is distracted by delight. She offers Him the skin of a banana and throws away the fruit. Lord Krishna takes the skin and eats it with relish. It was just what He wanted to eat! The banana skin, at that moment, is His favourite food ever!'

Nachiket: 'Friendship is a sanctuary … It is protection for His friend Draupadi. And guidance for Arjun.'

Lord Krishna has yet another friend—Draupadi. Also known as Krishnaa or Shyaama, she is the dark-skinned beauty who is wife to the Pandavas. He is there for her in her hour of need, when the Kuru court sits mute as Duhshasana drags her in their midst and attempts to disrobe her. But it is a futile attempt. For Lord Krishna keeps His friend enrobed. Endlessly enrobed.

And then there is Arjun, His ultimate friend. The one who finally makes himself ready for what he needs to hear, and not what he wants to hear. For till we are ready, guidance must wait. Love is patient.

Arjun is the one Lord Krishna teaches. The one to whom He chooses to reveal the secrets of life, death, action and inaction. Lord Krishna tells Arjun that He loves no one. And hates no one. Howsoever, love must triumph over attachment for life to thrive. He must yearn to unite and not dominate. Arjun learns this soon.

Lopamudra: 'If we wonder when Lord Krishna stops mollycoddling, soothing, testing, confusing ... When are we ready to listen and learn? Well, it is up to us.'

Nachiket: 'Sometimes love is the strength to discipline, forewarn or even punish. Like in Lord Krishna's treatment of Shishupala. Tough love.'

Anirban: 'Let me get this right. So, I must give a person ninety-nine chances to be wrong. And then come down on him—or her—with the wrath of a *Sudarshan Chakra*!'

'*You* are not Lord Krishna, Anirban,' Lopamudra laughed. 'Don't be so arrogant! Lord Krishna is Life.'

Anirban sat up straight. 'Wow! Lord Krishna is Life. Then I'm Shishupala! Who gets ninety-nine chances and then the thwack!'

Yudhishthira the Pandava is anointed king of Indraprastha. The grand ceremony is attended by luminaries from near and far. Friends gather, one and all, and so do enemies, one and all. At the forefront, the inimical Kaurava cousins.

The priests exhort that a guest of honour be selected. The Pandava brothers choose their friend and confidante, Lord Krishna of Dwaraka. As the most important guest ascends to the ceremonial pedestal, unrest spreads in a corner of the room.

Shishupala, the cowardly king of Chedi, steps up in a huff. He is offended with the choice. For there are many in the assembly who are more deserving of the honour, he is convinced. He proceeds now, to list the reasons why Lord Krishna is not worthy of the honour.

It is a litany of abuses and insults which emanate from envy and resentment. The Pandavas rise, affronted, ready to defend the honour of their special guest. Lord Krishna holds them back. For He has a plan to execute. And the time has come.

Shishupala is the son of His father's sister, and at his birth it is foretold that he will meet his end at the hands of his cousin, Lord Krishna. The aunt begs her nephew to forgive her son's misdemeanours. The divine nephew promises: I will forgive a hundred times. No more. No less.

Shishupala's tirade knows no bounds. In a flow, he continues, losing the vestiges of decency and decorum. Each insult is forgiven. Each affront is recorded.

The hundredth slander is hurled. Lord Krishna raises His hand and comes to His feet. He smiles. He warns. 'Cousin, you must stop now. My word has been kept. The next misdemeanour will come with a consequence. Be aware.'

Shishupala has lost all semblance of self-control. Seized by a blind rage, he spits out his next abomination. In a flash, Lord Krishna hurls His Sudarshan Chakra. Shishupala loses his enraged head.

Gargi: 'You can be Meera instead. Love can be a yearning.'

Lopamudra: 'Meera's love is also the path of solitude. A yearning for integration within; building a relationship between your worst and best self. Lord Krishna's *leela* (*enactment*) is about the life within us also.'

Gargi: 'What's the difference between Meera's love and Radha's love?'

Lopamudra continued. 'Well, Meera wants exclusivity. "*Mere toh Giridhar Gopal … Doosra na koi. Only me. Only you.*" Had Meera known inclusion, she would have seen her Lord Krishna in her husband, the Rana. And her Rana in her Lord Krishna. Radha knows inclusivity. She knows it *cannot* be only me!'

Gargi: '*Vedi Meera basli rusuni*
uposhanaala maandun aasan
nirjal tee maage tyaala
ekach te itkese aarzav
mhane kashi ti dolyaanni tya
raag bharuni vedya premacha
nakocha Radha nako Rukmini
Meera hi sarvasva poori!
Another one by Sneha Datar.[102] Translate, Nachiket!'
Nachiket laughed.
'*Ardent Meera sits in a sulk*
In penance, no food, no sprinkle of water
One, just this one appeal
Her eyes, they struggle to express
The pique of her fervid love:
No! No Radha, no Rukmini!
Just Meera! Enough, ample, all!'
Gargi: 'Lovely! I adore your translations!'

Nachiket winked at her and then looked at his mother-in-law. 'You would say that about Sudama and Arjuna also? Sudama wants to be *only me*, and Arjuna knows it cannot be *only me*?!'

Dharma Raj: 'I don't know about Sudama and Arjun, but some people are hurting and alone. They need to feel special. Exclusive. Others,' he looked at his wife, 'already know that they are special.'

Lopamudra: 'And, that everyone is special.'

Gargi: 'So, Papa, you are saying that it's a good idea to assuage and mollycoddle hurt, helpless people who do not know how to manage their own lives. Indulge the crazies instead of giving them a dose of good, clean sensible talk and shaking them up.'

Dharma Raj: 'People like you can always dish out the truth to one and all! The tribe of truth tellers!'

Nachiket: 'Gargi has an amazing quality. She can hear the uncomfortable truth about herself. Her problem is that she thinks everyone has that quality!'

Gargi laughed. 'Everyone should, *na*?!'

Lopamudra: 'There you go again. That tyrannical word—should!'

Dharma Raj: 'Do you aim to only have your say, or to achieve your goal? Would you like to help someone cope with life, or to only tell them how and why they are wrong?'

Gargi: 'And we help others by indulging their delusions, is it? By letting them believe what they want to believe?'

Lopamudra: 'The art of listening without judging is a most precious gift, Gargi. To listen to whatever a person has to say, without contradicting. Really, really, listen with empathy. To open your heart to someone, as if that person is your Meera. Your Sudama. By giving them the space to let it all out. "Bleeding out," Papa had called it once. It calms them down when they find validation for what they need to believe. They feel acknowledged. It reduces the noise in their head. You may then find a window to tell them what they need to hear! The Kairos moment.'

Gargi: 'And if you never find that window?'

Lopamudra: 'Well, then you are practising kindness. Giving solace. Soothing an aching heart. It's not such a bad thing, you know.'

Anirban: 'This is fascinating, what you guys have just said. You can really have power over that person, then. It can bring out wickedness in you.'

Lopamudra: 'Yes. Or divinity. Practising this kind of empathy can help you confront yourself as well. Are your intentions bona fide or mala fide? Why are you doing what you are doing? Are you helping? Giving solace? Are you enjoying the attention? Are you enjoying the devotion? Are you enjoying the drama? Is it this, or that? Or is it both? Your bona fide *and* mala fide? Your inner monster *and* hero?'

The Sanskrit play 'Urubhanga', written by Bhasa,[103] evocatively describes the final moments of Duryodhana, the great enemy of the Pandavas and the 'evildoer' in the great Indian epic, Mahabharata:

It is the eighteenth day of the Great Battle. The valiant Kaurava warriors—Bhishma, Drona, Karna—lie dead on the brutal fields of Kurukshetra. Ninety-nine Kaurava brothers are dead. Duryodhana, the eldest, is the last man standing.

A duel is offered to the vanquished man. Duryodhana picks his cousin Bhima as his final adversary and a mace as the weapon of choice. The brave warrior selects the toughest opponent. The combat begins and the warriors' maces clash. It is soon evident to the Pandava spectators that the encounter is an impasse. Lord Krishna signals to Bhima to hit Duryodhana on the thigh—his weak spot. The latter falls to the ground, mortally wounded. The felled warrior bemoans the unlawful blow. It is an unfair conduct in a mace fight.

Lord Krishna's elder brother Balarama walks up to Duryodhana and sits down beside his half-dead student; Balarama was Duryodhana's guru in mace warfare. The wounded man consoles his guru and asks him to shed his anger and forgive the Pandavas. He understands the futility of war now. He exhorts his cousins to accord his brothers an honourable cremation.

Duryodhana spots his parents, wives and children walking towards him slow-footed. He is unable to rise and touch the feet of his parents, who have lost their hundred sons. He consoles Gandhari and Dhritarashtra and asks them to be proud of their just, courageous warrior-son who will now be an honourable martyr. His heart breaks at his emasculated inability to console Malavi and Pauravi, his distraught wives. He exhorts them to honour his courage and celebrate the slain warrior.

He then addresses Durjaya, his young son. He asks him to obey grandmother Kunti and be respectful towards his Pandava uncles. Draupadi and Subhadra would heretofore be his mothers.

He attempts to calm the enraged Ashvatthama and reminds him of their Kaurava karma—their past acts: cheating at the game of dice, heinously humiliating Draupadi, cowardly slaying young Abhimanyu ...

Duryodhana looks at the light emanating from an unending tunnel. The warrior takes his last breath.

Urubhanga was written by the great Sanskrit playwright Bhasa more than two millennia ago. The great Indian playwright invokes the verisimilitude of Odin's Valhalla in the final moments of Duryodhana the warrior's death. No doubt Valkyries descend and escort him to Valhalla, the Nordic heaven for the greatest warriors.

A hero is sometimes also a controlled monster. Duryodhana the Monster could have been Suyodhana the Hero all the time, if only he had exhibited throughout his life the control that he showed at the time of his death.

Dharma Raj breathed in and leaned back. 'Well well well ... Lord Krishna gives us a template for all relationships: from Yashoda to Meera; Nanda to Arjuna; Sudama to Udhava; Shishupala to Kansa ... And the overarching lesson is to never lose the joy. Come what may. Relationships should be joyful, not heavy.'

Gargi: 'Heavy?'

Lopamudra: 'Emotionally chaotic. Relationships should be energy-giving, not energy-sucking. Only then will they be joyful. Like Lord Krishna's relationships.'

Anirban: 'Aunty, just for clarity, can you describe Goddess Laxmi and Lord Krishna's love?'

Lopamudra: 'Goddess Laxmi is the embodiment of being-love. Lord Krishna is the embodiment of expressed-love. Goddess Laxmi is fullness. Lord Krishna is joy.'

Nachiket: 'Fullness leads to joy. Emptiness makes you chase excitement, thrills, highs …'

Lopamudra: 'Yes. There is Goddess Laxmi's abundance in the Dalai Lama's exuberance. It is present in Lord Jesus's compassion and love for all. Their presence itself is joy and love. It needs no action. It's the sheer power of being … Lord Krishna-love is joy in connections.' She looked at Anirban, 'It's what you and Malivalaya can be, Anirban. What you and Nachiket can be, Gargi. What you and I can be, Raj.'

Dharma Raj: 'The archetypal image for Lord Krishna-love is a mother. My mother, your mother, the Dalai Lama's mother … It is Mother Mary and Yashoda.'

Nachiket cast a glance towards his mother-in-law. 'It's Lopamudra.'

Gargi's eyes welled up. 'Yes. It's Ma.'

14
THE GREAT DEVOTEE

THE GREAT DEVOTEE

D r Adarsh: 'Should we wind up for today?'

Anirban: 'Preferably not!'

Lopamudra: 'We do have a *puja* tomorrow. It's Ganesh Chaturthi.'

Anirban: 'I'd love to hear your views on the ritual of *puja*.'

Dharma Raj: 'Come over tomorrow. Attend a *puja*. Adarsh of course has a *puja* at home, but you can come here, Anirban.'

Dr Adarsh: 'My daughter's excitement has affected everybody in the house. Important guest is arriving tomorrow!'

Nachiket: 'Absolutely. But we cannot end the evening without discussing Bajrang Bali. Lord Hanumanji.'

Raavan kidnaps Goddess Sita and carries Her off to Lanka in his *pushpak vimaan* (*flower flying chariot*). He keeps Her confined in the precincts of *Ashok Vatika* (*the Forest of Ashok*); 'Ashok' is the *Saraca asoca* tree and its name literally translates to 'no grief'. Lord Ram prepares for battle and begins to garner an army. He asks His trusted companion Lord Hanuman to fly to Lanka and deliver a message of strength to His imprisoned wife. Lord Hanuman meets Goddess Sita, delivers the message from the husband to His wife, but is caught by the Lankan security forces and dragged into the presence of Raavan, enchained. Who could keep the great son of Vayu confined for long? He escapes and sets the Golden City of Lanka on fire before returning to His Lord and Master, Lord Ram.

Later, during the War of Lanka, Lord Lakshman is grievously wounded by Indrajit, son of Raavan. All efforts to revive him fail. The healers suggest that the Sanjeevani plant from Govardhan mountain will save Lord Ram's beloved brother. But who will bring this plant to the battlefield of Lanka?

Lord Hanuman flies off on this arduous journey. He lands on Govardhan mountain, but is confused and unable to identify the Sanjeevani plant. With no time to lose, He makes a swift decision and uproots the entire mountain. Holding it aloft in His right hand, He makes His return journey. Lord Lakshman is brought back to life.

Still later, Indrajit falls in battle and Raavan is blinded by grief. He reaches out to Ahiravana, the king of Patala Loka, the seventh realm of the netherworld, for help in defeating the army of Lord Ram. Ahiravana is an accomplished illusionist and master of hallucinations. He transforms himself into Vibhishana, Raavan's turncoat brother, and approaches the brothers Lord Ram and Lord

Lakshman. They unsuspectingly accompany him to the netherworld.

Lord Hanuman cottons on to the plot and speedily follows them, determined to rescue the two brothers. He arrives in the beguilingly enchanted Patala Loka and makes repeated attempts to find, locate and rescue the Ayodhyan brothers. Finally, He realizes that Ahiravana's invincibility is ensured by five eternal lamps placed far apart in five different directions. The skilled Pavanaputra, Lord Hanuman, transforms Himself and acquires five heads. He blows air in the direction of all the lamps at the same time and extinguishes them. Ahiravana dies, and Lord Ram and Lord Lakshman are rescued from the netherworld. Heretofore He is known as *Panchmukhi* (*the one with five faces*).[104]

Lord Hanuman is the epitome of devotion and physical, mental and emotional strength. He is the son of the Vanar King Kesari and Anjani, an *apsara* or *nymph*. Lord Vayu, the God of Wind, is also considered to be His father as He played a magical role in His birth.

He is known by various other names like Maruti, Anjaneya, Vayuputra, Kesarinandana, Mahabali, Vajranga, Pavanasuta and Anjanisuta. He is elder brother to the other famous son of Lord Vayu, Bhima the Pandava. The Shiva Purana gives Him the status of an *ansh* (*part*) of Lord Shiva.

Nachiket: 'Have you heard of the Sankat Mochan temple in Banaras?'

Dharma Raj: 'Of course. Tulsidasji wrote parts of the *Ramcharitmanas* in the temple premises.'

Nachiket: 'During my internship at the Clark's Hotel, I visited Sankat Mochan at least twice a week. I tried to make it for the morning *aarti* (*lamp lighting ritual*) if I could. No temple has moved me like this one did.'

Dr Adarsh: 'It's arguably among the most revered temples of Lord Hanuman in India.'

Dharma Raj: 'Certainly in Banaras.'

Nachiket: 'Have any of you been there?'

Dr Adarsh: 'I have; and the *aarti* is absolutely amazing.'

Nachiket: 'Let me describe it for the rest of you. So, the main sanctum sanctorum, of course, belongs to Lord Hanuman, the Supreme Devotee. People gather from 3 in the morning and wait for the massive doors to open. They open only after the pundits complete their rituals of awakening, bathing, and adorning the Lord. The doors are thrown open to the sound of cymbals and drums when He is ready, and we—the devotees of the Devotee, break out into ecstatic bhajans as we gaze at Him.'

Dharma Raj: 'But Lord Hanuman has eyes for another!'

Nachiket: 'So you know it, Papa. Yes, He does. On the other side of the main temple is a smaller temple. The two temples face one another. This other temple is of Lord Ram, His Master. Standing beside Him is His wife, Goddess Sita, and none of the gathered people face Lord Ram and His wife. It's amazing. The worshippers come for His most ardent follower: Lord Hanuman.'

Dharma Raj: 'They've come to acknowledge the disciple and celebrate discipleship.'

Anirban: 'Have they?'

Lopamudra: 'They have, knowingly or unknowingly. Spiritual experiences are subtle, Anirban. Your heart often knows what your mind does not.'

Nachiket: 'Meanwhile the doors of the temple of Lord Ram are opened, quietly and without fanfare, just after the doors of His Chief Devotee. The people continue to face the Devotee, not Lord Ram. Only Lord Hanuman is entitled to the first *darshan* (*view*) of the Lord.'

Gargi: 'You never told me this story, Nachiket. It's so beautiful. We face the Devotee because we need to learn what devotion is. Lord Hanuman breathes devotion.'

Nachiket: 'Lord Hanuman teaches us discipleship and devotion. Hopefully, we can all experience it.'

Anirban: 'What is discipleship? What is devotion?'

Dharma Raj: 'A true Disciple aims to mirror the Master. Devotion is emulation. First distill the qualities from the personality of the Master and then emulate the qualities. Sometimes we get lost in the emotions of the personalities of both the Master and the Disciple. That kind of devotion is based on *bhavna (feelings)*.'

Nachiket: 'This is the way I looked at the Sankat Mochan ceremony: Lord Ram is the *Maryada Purushottam*. And the first *view* of the *Ideal Follower of Laws* must be the privilege of one who personifies following the Right Path. So Lord Hanuman gets the first *darshan*. When the *puja* to the Disciple is over, the visitors turn their attention to Lord Ram. The route to *Dharma* is through discipleship. And Lord Hanuman is a disciple of *Dharma*.'

Dr Adarsh: 'What a wonderful ritual.'

Lopamudra: 'It throws an interesting light on the role of the guru as well. The teacher too is in search of Dharma, though sometimes a couple of strides ahead. Humility must be the central quality in the guru. Life is circular and he needs to keep the disciple in him alive. What better compliment can there be for a guru, than that one day he becomes the disciple, and his disciple becomes his guru?'

Dharma Raj laughed.

Nachiket: 'Humility would be difficult if someone is devoted to you. Anyone—man or woman.'

Lopamudra: 'It's best not to be on the receiving end of devotion. It's one of life's most challenging tests. It puts you on a slippery slope because it feeds the ego. It can push you into narcissism.'

Nachiket: 'What about devotion on the giving end?'

Lopamudra: 'Why not choose admiration instead? Admire, but question. Admire, but observe dispassionately. Experiencing devotion to a person is powerful if understood correctly. But it's very difficult to understand it correctly. Most people sink into emotions and psychological dependence. The emotional high becomes more important than emulating the guru. Lord Ram and Lord Hanuman offer important lessons—Lord Ram did not lose His steadiness and humility, despite receiving deep devotion. Lord Hanuman did not lose His strength, centredness and energy, despite being deeply devoted.'

Dharma Raj: '"Sankat Mochan" means the "Redeemer of Distress". We can deal with life's pressures with discipline and commitment, if we do what must be done without any ego. That's when consciousness moves a millimetre. Lord Hanuman attracts the disciplined and dutiful. Like my Nachiket.'

Nachiket smiled as he looked at his guru.

Gargi too smiled, her eyes brimming with love.

Lopamudra: 'There's more. Power must be tethered by love and humility. Otherwise, it is brutal. Lord Hanuman displays this in the image of His ripped chest.

Placed within His heart are the images of Siya Ram: Lord Ram and Goddess Sita.'

Dr Adarsh: 'His heart is the seat of steadfast love and surrender. He's the hero with strength, humility and devotion. He does not aspire for the spotlight.'

Gargi: 'You know, Lord Surya—the Sun God—taught Lord Hanuman *Pranayama* (*breath control*). True strength needs controlled, vibrant energy. No fuzziness. By worshipping Lord Hanuman, we learn to harness our own energies.'

Anirban: 'Lord Hanuman reminds me of Hercules, the Greco-Roman God-hero. But without the angst.'

Gargi: 'We must discuss Gods and Goddesses from other ancient cultures in detail someday. Greece ... and even Egypt.'

Anirban: 'Hmmm ... And find the parallels. Goddess Athena is the Goddess Saraswati of the Greeks, for instance. She carries the torch of wisdom and the arts. She is also the Goddess of Higher love.'

Dr Adarsh: 'What's Higher Love?'

Anirban: 'As opposed to lower, sensual love. Which is Goddess Aphrodite for the Greeks. Higher love is mental love. Lower love is physical, more desire-filled ... Goddess Isis is the Goddess Athena of Egypt. Goddess Bastet is the Goddess Aphrodite of Egypt.'

Nachiket: 'Isn't Goddess Athena also the Goddess of War? Then she is also Goddess Durga, right?'

Gargi: 'Hmmm ... tell us more, Anirban.'

Anirban: 'Okay. Let me think. The Greek God Apollo is like our Surya Deva. And the Egyptian Lord Amon.'

Dharma Raj: 'Describe Lord Apollo. Three words.'

Anirban: 'Truth. Order. Light.'

Dharma Raj: 'Surya Deva!'

Anirban: 'Modern Western philosophers have juxtaposed Lord Apollo with Lord Dionysus. Dionysus is the ebb and flow of emotion. That would be like our Chandra Deva, right, Aunty?'

Dharma Raj: 'Yes. But Chandra Deva is also Soma Deva.'

Anirban: 'And Soma is wine?'

Dharma Raj: 'Some people say so. Others disagree.'

Anirban: 'Well, Dionysus is the God of Wine. And intuition. And exuberance.'

Nachiket: 'Fascinating.'

Anirban: 'Lord Osiris is like Lord Krishna in some aspects, as in "path-giver". And the God Horus, His son, is His Arjuna.'

Gargi: 'Listen, they are all fascinating and we will talk about them too someday, but Anirban, tell us about Narcissus. He's the God of Narcissism, I presume?!'

Dr Adarsh: 'God of Narcissism? That's precious!'

Narcissus is impossibly handsome, a sight to joyfully behold. He is the son of Cephissus, a river God and Liriope, a nymph.

Echo, a mountain nymph, falls hopelessly in love with him. But she has been cursed by Hera and can only repeat what is said to her.

In essence, she can only return what is directed to her!

Narcissus rejects her love. For he comes upon a spring and gazes at his reflection in the water, falling madly in love with himself! Indeed, he is beautiful to behold!

He pines. He moans. He sighs. He smiles. He cannot move. He cannot touch, for with every attempted contact he disturbs the water and vanishes out of sight! He dies, gazing upon himself. Mesmerized. Enchanted.

Narcissus, the flower, springs to life at the spot where the man, at last, stops breathing.[105]

Dharma Raj: 'Beautiful. Beguiling. Frightening!'

Nachiket: 'There is a Narcissus in us all. We love ourselves. Tell me, Gargi, when you look at a photograph that also has you, who do you first look at? Hypothetically, let us say there is a photo of you, me and Amitabh Bachchan. Who will you look at first?'

Gargi: 'Me. First myself. Then you. Then Amitabh Bachchan!'

Nachiket: 'I love your honesty. I don't know many who would readily admit such things! I wouldn't, especially when I'm with people I do not know well enough.'

Gargi: 'It's even less likely that you would admit such a thing with people you know well!'

Nachiket laughed softly.

Lopamudra: 'Interesting that Gargi said it would be first her, then you. And then Amitabh Bachchan. She did not say "only me". There are those who would look at only themselves. Those are narcissists.'

Dharma Raj: 'Or those who will only look at themselves with love and all others with scrutiny. Size them up.'

Lopamudra: 'Hmmm … Looking at myself with my heart-eye and everyone else with my head-eye. Narcissus.'

Anirban: 'Doesn't the world need that? It's not a pretty picture out there. We can't be suckers.'

Dharma Raj: 'We can learn to look with both the head and heart. At ourselves also. At ourselves first, actually. Scrutiny and kindness are rewarding when applied together. Distinctly non-Narcissus.'

Dr Adarsh: 'I worry about the times we live in. I worry about my daughter. Social media platforms are designed to create anxious narcissists. You're constantly seeking validation, approval and dominance. All of us have a little

Narcissus within us and today's technology can tip the balance. It's the children I worry about.'

Lopamudra: 'It's tough, yes. Thank God we didn't have to deal with all this when we were raising you, Gargi. But Adarsh, children—little children especially—they learn from imitation. They do what you do. Not what you say. Lead by example. You don't want your child to watch too much TV? You don't watch too much TV! You want your child to read books? Let her see you reading books. You don't want your child to stick to her phone? You don't stick to yours! But most importantly, make your child feel secure, safe, loved. Teach your child how to recognize and regulate emotions ... Having said that, I know it's tough being a parent today. One does not have enough control over the variables!'

Dharma Raj: 'The most important thing you can do for your child is to love your spouse. Mumma loves Papa. Papa loves Mumma. And Mumma and Papa love me.'

Lopamudra: 'But don't lose sight of how to love. To love is to accept. To love is to give. Not take. To not want to extract. Not try and change. Not try and "reform". "I love you. I must fix you!" That is not love. We are too focused on what we are getting. Not on what we are giving or doing or being in a relationship.'

Dr Adarsh felt helpless and enraged. 'How much do you give, without ever receiving?'

Lopamudra: 'You learn to receive what is given, Adarsh.'

The air was suddenly heavy. Nachiket gently got up and sat beside Dr Adarsh. Quietly.

'Lord Krishna-love! Not Narcissus-love!' Gargi trilled.

Nachiket smiled softly. His Gargi, who did not really register people or see them beyond the surface. Believing that what she saw on the surface was all there is. Untouched and unthreatened by life. Heartbreakingly beautiful. Strangely insensitive. Unnaturally innocent. So innocent …

'Narcissists can be high-achievers,' Anirban took the discussion forward. 'They can do well in life. They know how to put themselves before others.'

Dharma Raj: 'Controlled narcissism can be useful, yes. But it empties you emotionally. You will not be content. Deep down you will be quite alone and lonely.'

Lopamudra: 'Echo was his opportunity. I loved that bit about Echo, Anirban. Echo mirrors what you give. So, had Narcissus loved her with that intensity he kept only for himself, he would have received it in return. Life echoes what you give it.'

Anirban: 'Reminds me of Lord Jesus Christ and His message of love.'

Dharma Raj: 'Christianity and Islam have accumulated mysticism and symbolic messaging over time.'

Lopamudra: 'Yes ... Although they began as socio-political movements.'

Dharma Raj: 'Lopa, religions that began as mystical, inner experiences over time acquired socio-political overtones, didn't they?'

Lopamudra: 'What are you trying to say?'

Dharma Raj: 'I'm saying that both politics and imagination are essential human traits. Over time, those religions with politics at their core sprouted mystical streams, and those with mystery and Nature at their core found political expression.'

Dr Adarsh: 'What do you mean by religions with politics at their core?'

Dharma Raj: 'Adarsh, this needs to be another discussion altogether. We discussed it a bit, in the hospital the other day. You were not there. I promise we'll do it one day. All I'll say now is that politics isn't necessarily a bad word. And in this case, I'm talking about those religions which began as social reform movements, like Islam and Christianity. It was good politics.'

Lopamudra: 'I keenly look forward to this conversation.'

Nachiket: 'It'll be the day when Ma and Papa lock horns!'

Dharma Raj: 'Today's not that day, for sure. Anyway, coming back to Christianity. Lord Jesus resonates with grace, love, forgiveness and sacrifice.'

Dr Adarsh: 'And service, Uncle. I did my residency in CMC, Vellore. They're God-fearing, the Christians. And their commitment to the service of humanity is unparalleled. No doubt.'

Anirban: 'In September 2016, I found myself at the feet of Christ the Redeemer in Lisbon. I was going through a personal crisis at the time. I remember looking up to His image and asking Him, what am I being called upon to sacrifice, or forgive?'

Nachiket: 'You did?'

Anirban: 'Most unlike me, I admit. But we all have our moments. Anyway, Lord Jesus astounded me with His answer: "Sacrifice your fears and doubts. Forgive the person who has hurt you and cast aside your pain. Embrace the one you love. And then fly. You are free!" I returned to India and married Malivalaya.'

Gargi: 'Wow, Anirban. It was unlike you to say that so easily.'

Anirban smiled.

Nachiket: 'Sufi Islam also developed as a brand of mystical magic and divine intoxication.'

Lopamudra: 'That's true. Jalaluddin Rumi is my favourite …

Why should I seek more?
I am the same as He.
His essence speaks through me.
I have been looking for myself.[106]'

Nachiket: 'I love qawwalis as well.'

Lopamudra: 'They clean your cells of emotional debris!'

Nachiket: 'Just like bhajans, hymns and kirtans. They can drive Gargi to delirium!'

Gargi: 'Sufism. Reminds me of Sehvan. Sindh. Lord Jhulelal.'

Punjab Sindh Gujarat Maratha
Dravida Utkala Banga ...

Precious for over a billion people, these words have been plucked from the Indian National Anthem. Diana Eck calls India 'a Sacred Geography'.[107] Indeed, it is, for one among the regions named in those lines is notional. The territory of Sindh lies, today, in Pakistan. Not India. And yet, it has not been dropped from our anthem. It will never be dropped. For it honours a displaced people. The Sindhi Hindu migrants from West Pakistan.

Sindh. The land that flanks the mighty River Sindhu, also known as River Indus. It is the cradle of Indian civilization. It lives through the invasion of Alexander the Great and, having faced wave after wave of attacks, this hardy land finally falls to the sword of Mohammed bin Qasim in 712 CE, during the reign of King Dahir.[108]

After a succession of Muslim rulers, the region comes under the rule of the fanatical Mirk Shah in the mid-tenth century. He decrees that all Hindus living in his region must embrace Islam immediately. The vexed Sindhis turn to *Mahajans*, the *wise men* of the community, who suggest that they find sanctuary at the feet of Lord Varuna, God of the Waters. They congregate on the banks of *Ma Sindhu* (*Mother Indus*).

They sing songs. They chant His name. They pray for forty days. And then their prayers are answered. An *akashvani* (*Divine Voice/Message from the Sky*) exhorts them to take heart. An *avatar* will be born in Nasarpur to Ma Devki in the house of Ratan Raj. Mirk Shah hears of the proclamation and has the matter investigated. Indeed, a child is born to Ma Devki on Chaitra Beej; the second day of the month of Chaitra in Shukla Paksha, the waxing moon period.

Uderolal. Jhulelal. Avatar of Lord Varuna.

Mirk Shah summons the community and orders that they convert without delay. They refuse. Their Lord has arrived. They will be protected. Mirk Shah orders that the child be killed. His *vazir* (*minister/adviser*) Ahiro travels to Nasarpur and visits the house of Ratan Raj. The delighted father obliges the man who carries with him a rose. Alas, the flower has been dunked in poison. Ahiro moves close to the cradle. The gurgling child blows at the flower. The petals fly and fall at the feet of the vazir. Even as he watches, bemused, he sees a vision of the child transfiguring into an old man with a flowing white beard who rides away, holding a sword aloft. The other hand carries a flag. Heretofore, Ahiro is a devotee of the river God.

He returns to Mirk Shah. The king is now afraid. He decides to wait and watch ... Ma Devki passes on. Ratan Raj remarries. The child is a young boy now. He loves the Sindhu. He plays with the children. Distributes beans. Comforts the sick. Talks to the grown-ups. He even gives offerings to the Great River. The river gives Him back a bowl of rice.

Mirk Shah is advised by his clerics to speed up the conversion of the locals. He decides he must meet the 'Divine One'. Ahiro advises him that Allah of the Muslims and Ishwar of the Hindus are one. Lord Jhulelal is the same as Khwaja Khirz.

Mirk Shah orders that Uderolal be imprisoned. Giant waves prevent the arrest. The soldiers drown. Fire breaks out in the palace ... Mirk Shah is finally transformed. Jubilant Hindus build a temple to the Lord. Lord Jhulelal to them is now water and light personified.

Lord Jhulelal designates His cousin Pugar Sahib as the first *Thakur*, *priest* to His People, the Dariya Panthi. The people of the Water God. Lord Jhulelal gives the First Priest seven sacred symbols: Deg the Cooking Vessel, Teg the Sword, Jyot the Sacred Fire, Mudra the Divine Ring,

Jal ki Jhari the Divine Water Pot, Khintha the Sacred Cloth and Cheera the Headgear.

Lord Jhulelal drops His body as Hindus and Muslims observe the sacred event. A heavenly voice declares that a shrine be built, its one face a temple and the other a dargah shrine.

To this day, He remains a unifying force. Adored by Hindus. Adored by Muslims. Dariyalal to the Lohanas. Zinda Pir to the Muslims. Mast Qalandar to the Sufis ...

'Jhulelal, Bera hi Paar,' the Sindhis murmur as they meet. Lohanas exclaim, 'Jai Jhulelal.'

Gargi reached for her phone and once again paired it with the speaker. 'On that note, I present to you the Sindhi mystic, Lal Shahbaz Qalandar. In the voice of Runa Laila ...

O...ho...O...ho...

Ho Lal Meri Pat Rakhiyo Bala Jhoolelaalan
Sindhri Da Sehvan Da Sakhi Shabaaz Qalandar
Duma Dum Mast Qalandar, Ali Da Pehla Number ...

O Red-robed Lord, Protect me, Jhulelalan,
Friend of Sindh, Friend of Sehwan,
Glory to you, Shahbaz Qalandar, the Number One ...'

15

THE LORD OF THE
PEOPLE ARRIVES

Gargi and Nachiket had stayed over at the Deshpande residence. The morning began like any other, early but lazy. Dharma Raj made ginger tea for his family, and they sat in the veranda in silence. The strains of Raga Lalit wafted in from the living room. In good time, Lopamudra got up and walked indoors. That one act changed the tempo of the house—from *ati vilambit laya* to *drut laya*.

Muhurat (*the auspicious time*) was to begin at nine in the morning. The family was bathed and ready by eight.

Puranik Kaku, the priestess, arrived as the clock struck nine. The family gathered in the puja room and sat in a semicircle on the floor, after Puranik Kaku took her seat. Lopamudra informed her that she had already performed the regular *puja*. As Puranik Kaku placed the *paat* (*wooden base*), Anirban raced into the house after leaving his sandals in the veranda. He slowed his footsteps as he entered the puja room and quietly sat on the floor next to Nachiket.

Puranik Kaku began the Ganesh Pratishthapana. She spread rice grains on the *paat* and placed the Ganesh idol on it. A *sankalp* (*resolution*) was taken: she pronounced that she would now undertake the Parthiv Ganesh pujan vrata as laid down by the shrutis, smritis and Puranas. She offered a kalash, shankh, ghant and diya to the Lord. She offered gandha and flowers.

The main ritual of Pran-pratishtha began. She applied ghee to the Lord's eyes using the Durva grass. She placed her thumb on the Lord's heart and recited mantras, inducing life in the idol. She performed the *shodash upchaars* (*sixteen formalities*).

Lopamudra and Nachiket had cooked the *Naivedya* (*offering*): twenty-one ukadeecha modaks, along with varan bhaat, limbu tup, polya, batatyachi bhaaji, kakdichi koshimbir, papad, lonache and taak. Two well-laid thalis had been placed by the side of Puranik Kaku. She offered one plate to all the Gods and Goddesses in the puja ghar, and the other to the chief guest, Lord Ganesh.

On Puranik Kaku's indication, the *aarti* began …

Sukhkarta Dukhharta Varta Vighnachi || Nurvi Purvi Prem Krupa Jayachi ||

Sarvangi Sundar Uti Shendurachi || Kanti Jhalke Mal Mukataphalaanchi ||

Jaidev Jaidev Jai Mangal Murti || Darshan Maatre Man Kaamna Purti ||

Ratnakhachit Phara Tujh Gaurikumra || Chandanaachi Uti Kumkumkeshara ||

Hirejadit Mukut Shubhato Bara || Runjhunati Nupure Charani Ghagriya ||

Jaidev Jaidev Jai Mangal Murti || *Lambodar Pitaambar Phanivarvandana* ||

Saral Sond Vakratunda Trinayana || *Das Ramacha Vat Pahe Sadana* ||

Sankati Pavave Nirvani Rakshave Survarvandana ||

Jaidev Jaidev Jai Mangal Murti ||

Everyone bowed to the Lord. The prasad was distributed and the ceremony ended.

Dharma Raj and Anirban moved to the living room. Lopamudra thanked Puranik Kaku and escorted her to the gate. Gargi and Nachiket entered the kitchen to make some tea ...

16

THE MAGIC OF CEREMONY

Anirban: 'That was a moving experience. Thank you, Aunty and Uncle.'

Dharma Raj: 'You're welcome, Anirban. I'm glad you felt the magic.'

Anirban: 'I did. My mother would have been happy today. My father would be shocked!'

Dharma Raj: '*Puja* is the most popular and mass-based divine practice. It is the first step. When it's performed in a group, it creates bonding and fraternity. Like it did right now. When you do it alone, it inculcates *dhyaan*.'

Anirban: '*Attention*?'

Dharma Raj: 'Yes. It makes us focus on the current moment. It pulls us away from the past and future and brings us to the present. And in the present, attention decides which stimulus registers with us; and, therefore, our response.'

There was a sudden sound of screeching wheels.

Nachiket nodded toward the sound. 'Sometimes it's not in our control, is it?'

Lopamudra walked into the room. 'True. Often it is unintended. But it doesn't have to be so. Our reality is determined by what we *choose* to see, hear or smell. It defines the way we experience life. So, we must learn to consciously choose what we pay attention to.'

Dharma Raj: 'It is very difficult to keep our attention focused. The monkey mind loves to waver. It is constantly pulled into the past—real or imagined—and then pushed into a future flight of fancy.'

Lopamudra: 'Well, fantasies are enchanting, dreams energize and nostalgia is absolutely wonderful! "Yesterday" and "tomorrow" are equally attractive. Isn't it interesting that Hindi has the same word for both?'

Dharma Raj: '"Kal". And, "*kal*" is rooted in "kaal" (time). Only the present moment—*aaj* and *abhi* (*today* and *now*)—has timeless significance. It deserves exclusive acknowledgement.'

Anirban: 'That's the most innovative take I have heard on the illogical anomaly of "yesterday" and "tomorrow" being the same word in Hindi! *Tussi* great *ho*!'

Lopamudra: 'It's not a facetious point, Anirban. It needs careful pondering.'

Nachiket and Gargi walked into the room, Gargi holding a tray laden with steaming teacups. She handed each person their cups and sat on a floor cushion, holding her cup with both hands.

Nachiket: 'True that. But even if the present moment becomes vivid, often it's because of our biases and tendencies. Or because of fears and doubts.'

Dharma Raj: 'Or what appeals to our senses. We need to practise focussing on the "right" thoughts, emotions, and events. It's an art. Pay attention *consciously*. Give up habits, resist distractions, just *make an effort*. *Puja*, the ceremony of rituals, is designed as a training ground for this possibility.'

Gargi: 'It certainly injects magic into the mundane!'

Dharma Raj smiled. 'Any ceremony is essentially a series of acts that are performed with awareness. If this awareness becomes second nature to us, then life itself can be lived like a ceremony.'

Lopamudra: 'Papa even bathes like it's a ceremony!'

Nachiket: 'The universe lives with ceremony. It's a living example of order. It's magic.'

Anirban: 'Not always.'

Nachiket: 'Yes, not always. There's chaos in Nature. But these disruptions are resets in the pursuit of balance. And I'm pretty sure the universe will get there before us humans!'

Lopamudra: 'We're a part of the universe, Nachiket. We're not separate. The universe isn't getting anywhere without us humans riding along … Anyway, a *puja* has a definite shape and is conducted in a specified order. It requires our undivided attention. In fact, a *puja* has tools that are designed to prevent our mind from wandering.'

Nachiket: 'I don't know about the undivided attention part, but I clearly remember the sequence of rituals in my *Aaji's* (*grandmother's*) daily *puja*. Her *puja* really emerged from her heart.'

Gargi: 'Tell us about it.'

Nachiket: 'Okay. As you all know, the Devis and Devatas in the puja ghar are revered guests, honoured with utmost hospitality. Every morning she spent two hours blissfully catering to them. We sat in a semi-circle around her ...'

Gargi: '"We" as in?'

Nachiket: 'Her grandchildren. She lovingly awakened each deity; bathed them: first with water, then with milk, then again with water. Then she towelled, clothed and covered them with tiny jewels ...'

Gargi: 'Jewels, meaning?'

Nachiket: 'Earrings, bangles, nose rings, necklaces, paayals ... the works. Then she seated them on their pedestals. She made the chandan paste and smeared it on their foreheads. She placed flowers at their feet. Then she served them food with honour; she scooped each tiny morsel carefully and raised it to their lips.'

Anirban: 'How sweet. And then?'

Nachiket: 'Well, then the Gods settled themselves in comfort for the rituals that followed!'

Gargi: 'Like?'

Nachiket: 'She drew either a *yantra* or *rangoli* on the cleaned patch of floor. Then carefully placed assorted items on the pattern.'

Gargi: 'You remember the items?'

Nachiket smiled. 'A paan leaf, betel nuts, flowers, tulsi, bilva leaves, sindoor, rice grains, camphor, incense sticks, diyas … the formation of the *yantra* and the items changed cyclically.'

Gargi: 'Based on?'

Nachiket: 'Ma?'

Lopamudra: 'It's determined by the time of day, moon phase and sun cycle. Continue, Nachiket.'

Nachiket: 'Thanks, Ma. Finally, she read a passage from some scripture, usually the *Ramcharitmanas*. She would explain to us as she went along. Then it would be time for the best part, what we waited for. The *aarti*! Bells and cymbals were handed to the children, and we rang them with thrill and gusto. Praises were sung to the Gods as the *aarti thali* was circulated and then passed around. It would begin with *Aaji*, then our parents and kakas and kakis and aatyas and everybody present. Finally, us, the grandchildren.'

Anirban: 'In strict order of precedence.'

Lopamudra: 'As it should be! And then the prasad?'

Nachiket: 'And then the prasad! I loved the *paanchaamrut* … That ended the ceremony.'

Lopamudra: 'Magic would fade into the invisible …'

Gargi: 'I remember *Aajoba's (grandfather's) pujas*. They were solemn and alone. Papa told me he practised dhyana.'

Lopamudra: 'That's right. He explored the inner world, and his tools were meditation and pranayama. He used mystical *yantras*. Many were mathematical.'

Gargi: 'I remember that! Papa, you had explained one to me: the *Kuber Kolam*.[109] To me it was a math puzzle. You told me it's a magic square.'

Dr Adarsh: 'What's a magic square?'

Gargi: 'It's a square grid of numbers in which all the rows, columns, and diagonals add up to the same value.'

Anirban: 'Oh! Wow! Amish's symbology never ends! I don't know if you guys registered it, but this *Kuber Kolam*, then, is depicted on the steps in the cover of his book, *Immortal India*.'

Gargi: 'Seriously? Let me get the book!'

Gargi rushed indoor and returned in a couple of minutes. 'You're right! 27, 20, 25 ... 22, 24, 26 ... 23, 28, 21 ... 27, 22, 23 ... 20, 24, 28 ... 25, 26, 21 ... 27, 24, 21 ... 25, 24, 23 ... They all add up to 72! I'm sure you knew, Papa!'

Dharma Raj smiled. 'Somehow the *Kuber Kolum* was a portal to self-awareness and cosmic unity for your *Aajoba*. During the Diwali *puja* he made a different magic square; he called it the *Laxmi Chautis Yantra*[110].'

Lopamudra: 'Gargi, you remember the time *Aajoba* visited this house, when we had just moved in? He'd done the *Pran-prathishtha* ceremony.'

Gargi: 'Yes, I clearly remember. The *Gods were brought to life*!'

Nachiket: 'Tell us about it. Let's see how much *you* remember!'

Gargi: 'Okay. In some ways it was like your *Aaji's puja*, Nachiket, but with more protocol and seriousness. Even grandeur. So, he first recited a lot of *Vaidic* mantras. Then the *adhivaas* (*abode*) of the Gods was established in our puja ghar. They were bathed, adorned and fed, just like you described. The *pancharatna* were kept at their feet.'

Anirban: '*Pancharatna* is *five gems*. But which ones?'

Gargi looked at her Papa.

Dharma Raj: 'Ruby, diamond, pearl, coral and yellow sapphire. Go on, Gargi. I'm amazed you remember the details.'

Gargi: 'I was sixteen, Papa. Old enough to remember. Anyway, then *Aajoba* touched the body parts of the Gods with a gold leaf.'

Dharma Raj: 'Breathing life into them …'

Gargi: 'Yes … he did this while chanting mantras— which I still don't understand the meaning of. He placed the gold leaf on each eye, and then, the spot between the eye: the third eye.'

Lopamudra: 'The third eye is the eye of intuition.'

Gargi: 'Hmmm … He told me the Gods had now become our consecrated *achal atithis* (*guests who will not move*).'

Nachiket: 'Man had breathed the life force of Godhood into the Gods.'

Anirban: 'That's very powerfully put, Nachiket. You just gave me goosebumps.'

Dharma Raj: 'What did you make of what Nachiket just said, Anirban?'

Anirban: 'That in fundamental terms, there is no difference between man and God. At our highest level, we are one. Like you said, Uncle; Plato's words: "Know thyself."'

Nachiket: 'Realize your potential Godhood. Become it.'

Lopamudra: 'Let me put it simply: *puja* is sacred. Use it to sharpen your attention and elevate your consciousness. Bond with others. Experience magic ... Either bring meaning to it, or don't do it at all.'

Dharma Raj: 'And if possible, for a moment maybe, experience stillness and wonder. There is no "other". But there is no "sameness" either. Just the one in the many.'

EPILOGUE

We live in thrall of Reason in current times. Reason is a potent tool in life but thraldom towards it limits a holistic experience of life. A rejoicing heart or a magical encounter with beauty may confound logical explanation, but it's possible to intuit its value. Human reason has galloped ahead, leaving behind the dwarfed sapling of wonder, wisdom and awe. The latter softens our outlook and makes life worth living. And it's a faculty that can be developed. The tools are available in the mythology and symbols bequeathed by ancient men and women.

Throughout the ages, idol-rejecters have wreaked havoc in their zeal to obliterate idolatry from planet Earth. Tens of millions of idol-worshippers have been killed, thousands of temples destroyed, tens of universities burnt to the ground and entire civilizations annihilated.

This was, almost certainly, the biggest genocide in human history, spread over more than 1,500 years. It continues to this day in countries like Pakistan.[111] Religious doctrine has camouflaged the prejudiced urge to dominate and spread one's influence over 'others'. This tribal urge is universal. Life seeks to expand, politically or otherwise. It is interesting though, that historically, there are very few examples of idol-worshipping civilizations seeking to destroy idol-rejecting cultures *because they reject idol worship*! Historically, almost everywhere that the idol-worshippers fought idol-rejectors over the last 1,500 years, it was a defensive war—a battle to survive, not to dominate and convert.

Idol-worshipping cultures are far from perfect. There is no perfection after all. But theological liberalism is one of the innate strengths of idol-worshipping cultures. We can learn this from idol-worshipping. If we truly see God in everything, it is impossible for us to hate anything. Because whatever you hate, will also have God within. It is no surprise then that idol-worshipping cultures have usually accommodated atheism as well. Idol-rejecting cultures, on the other hand, have struggled historically with atheism.

Whether we seek divinity within us or outside us, or we do not seek it at all, our experience of life will enhance with the grace of a few words: kindness, regard and the gift of an open mind.

NOTES

1. Catherine Nixey, *The Darkening Age: The Christian Destruction of the Classical World* (London: Macmillan Publishers, 21 September 2017).
2. Lunisolar calendar is the science on which Kaal Nirnays—the Hindu calendars—are based.
3. *Sakal* is a Marathi-language daily newspaper by Sakal Media Group. The headquarter is in Pune, Maharashtra, India.
4. Sarvajanik Ganesh Mandals or Sarvajanik Mandals are a social group that comes together to publicly celebrate Ganeshotsav. They usually put up a temporary tent-like temple, and decorate it with beautiful scenes from history, or geographical or man-made wonders. The arrival and *visarjan* of Lord Ganesh is a celebration with drums, dance and decor. A big beautiful *vigraha* of Lord Ganesh is established for daily ritual worship. *Aratis*, *pujas*, special *abhishekas*, Ganesh *atharvashirsha* recitals and cultural programmes are conducted on a daily basis. Social service activities like blood donation camps, public

lectures, etc., are also organized. In big cities like Mumbai and Pune, there are special and old traditional mandals that are called Maanaache Ganapati, and these have precedence in *pujas* as well as *visarjan* activities.

5. Amish, 'Lessons from PK: Beliefs may be cast in stone', 8 January 2015,
https://www.hindustantimes.com/columns/lessons-from-pk-beliefs-may-be-cast-in-stone/story-CqOufZDvC5xlACU6w6pEiN.html.

6. https://greekcitytimes.com/2021/06/27/olive-tree-acropolis/
https://www.britannica.com/topic/Athena-Greek-mythology
Stephan Weaver, *Greek Gods: The Olympians* (California: CreateSpace Independent Publishing Platform, September 2015).

7. Deuteronomy 12:3 (King James edition) 'And ye shall overthrow their altars, and break their pillars, and burn their groves with fire; and ye shall hew down the graven images of their Gods, and destroy the names of them out of that place.'
Commandment to Moses in Exodus 20:3
'Thou shalt have no other Gods before me.'
Deuteronomy 13:6 to 10
'If thy brother, the son of thy mother, or thy son, or thy daughter, or the wife of thy bosom, or thy friend, which is as thine own soul, entice thee secretly, saying, Let us go and serve other Gods, which thou hast not known, thou, nor thy fathers; 13:6
Namely, of the Gods of the people which are round about you, nigh unto thee, or far off from thee, from the one end of the earth even unto the *other* end of the earth; 13:7

Thou shalt not consent unto him, nor hearken unto him; neither shall thine eye pity him, neither shalt thou spare, neither shalt thou conceal him; 13:8

But thou shalt surely kill him; thine hand shall be first upon him to put him to death, and afterwards the hand of all the people.13:9

And thou shalt stone him with stones, that he die; because he hath sought to thrust thee away from the LORD thy God, which brought thee out of the land of Egypt, from the house of bondage.13:10'

8. Catherine Nixey, *The Darkening Age: The Christian Destruction of the Classical World* (London: Macmillan Publishers, 21 September 2017).

9. Ed. Andrew G. Bostom, MD, *The Legacy of Jihad: Islamic Holy War and the Fate of Non-Muslims*, chapter 52 (New York: Prometheus Books).

   Rowena Robinson, 'Some Neglected Aspects of the Conversion of Goa: A Socio-Historical Perspective', *Sociological Bulletin*, Vol. 42, No. 1/2 (March–September 1993), pp. 65-83, Sage Publications, Inc., https://www.jstor.org/ stable/23620248.

   Paul Axelrod and Michelle A. Fuerch, *Flight of the Deities: Hindu Resistance in Portuguese Goa*, pp. 387–421, Modern Asian Studies, May, 1996, Vol. 30, No. 2 (May, 1996), (New York: Cambridge University Press) https://www. jstor.org/stable/313013.

10. Francis Clark Murgotten, *The Origins of The Islamic State Being A Translation From The Arabic Accompanied With Annotations Geographic And Historical Notes Of The Kitab Futuh Al-Buldan Of al-Imam abu-l 'Abbas Ahmad ibn-Jabir al-Baladhuri* (New York: Columbia University, 1924), pp. 226–7.

11. Sita Ram Goel, *Hindu Temples: What Happened To Them, Volume II*, Appendix 4,The Islamic Evidence, Questionnaire For The Marxist Professors, pp. 408–422. 'The Emerging National Vision', Speech delivered by Sita Ram Goel on December 4, 1983 at Calcutta.

12. Tr. John Briggs, *Tarikh-i-Firishta*, translated into English by John Briggs under the title *History of the Rise of the Mahomedan Power in India, 4 Volumes*, (New Delhi Reprint, 1981).

    'The king acknowledged that there might be reason in what they said (to accept money from the infidels if the king would desist from iconoclasm), but replied, that if he should consent to such a measure, his name would be handed down to posterity as "Mahmood the idol-seller", whereas he was desirous of being known as "Mahmood the destroyer of idols" [but shikan]: he therefore directed the troops to proceed in their work.'

    Amir Khusrow writes in *Miftahu'l-Futuh* about Sultan Alau'd-Din Khalji (AD 1296–1316) and his generals conquest in Jhain (in Rajasthan): 'Many strong temples which would have remained unshaken even by the trumpet blown on the Day of Judgment, were levelled with the ground when swept by the wind of Islam (…) A cry rose from the temples as if a second Mahmud had taken birth'.

    Tr. Sir Jadu-Nath Sarkar, *Maasir-I-Alamgiri: A History of the Emperor Aurangzeb–'Alamgir (reign 1658–1707 AD) of Saqi Must'ad Khan,* (Calcutta: Royal Asiatic Society of Bengal, 1947).

    Inscription on mosque on the right hand side of the Ganesa Gate in the fort at Gwalior. Alexander

Cunningham, *Archaeological Survey of india, Four Reports Made During the Years 1862–63–64–65*:

'In the reign of the great Prince Alamgir, Like the full shining moon, The enlightener of the world, Was by Motamid Khan completed as an alms. It was the idol temple of the vile Gwali, He made it a mosque, like a mansion of paradise. (...) He closed the idol temple: Exclamations rose from earth to heaven, When the light put far away the abode of darkness (...)'.

Inscription on mosque at Bodhan, Andhra Pradesh, mentioned in Epigraphia Indo-Moslemica, 1919–1920 which is quoted from S.R. Goel, *Hindu Temples: What Happened to Them. Vol. II*:

'In obedience to the commandment of the Almighty God, the Lord of both the worlds; and in love of (...) the exalted Prophet: During the reign of Shahjahan, the king of seven climes, the viceregent of God (lit. Truth), the master of the necks of people (...) the benevolent and generous Prince Aurangzeb, whose existence is a blessing of the Merciful God on people: He built a house for worship with (all) the qualities of heaven: after the site has been previously occupied by the temple of infidels (...)'.

Niccolo Manucci, *Storia do Mogor Vol. 3*:

'In the realm of India, although King Aurangzeb destroyed numerous temples, there does not thereby fail to be many left at different places, both in his empire and in the territories subject to the tributary princes. All of them are thronged with worshippers; even those that are destroyed are still venerated by the Hindus and visited for the offering of alms. (...) The chief temples destroyed by king Aurangzeb within his kingdom were the following: Maisa (Mayapur)

Matura (Mathura)

Caxis (Kashi)

Hajudia (Ajudhya)

And an infinite number of others; but, not to tire the readers, I do not append the names'.

'Aurangzeb did this for two reasons: first, because by this time his treasures had begun to shrink owing to expenditure on his campaigns; secondly, to force the Hindus to become Mahomedans, to obtain relief from the insults of the collectors'.

Jadunath Sarkar quotes Aurangzeb's Akhbarat of 1705, in *History of Aurangzeb Vol. 3*:

'The Emperor, summoning Muhammad Khalil and Khidmat Rai, the darogha of hatchet-men (…) ordered them to demolish the temple of Pandharpur, and to take the butchers of the camp there and slaughter cows in the temple (…) It was done'.

Inscription of Mosque in Cuddapah, Andhra Pradesh from *Epigraphia Indo-Moslemica, 1937–38*:

'Although the king of the time [Aurangzeb] is not a prophet, yet there is no doubt in his being a friend of God. He built the mosque and broke the idols (at a time) when 1103 years had passed from the flight (of the Prophet).'

Ali Muhammad Khan, *Mirat-i-Ahmadi*:

'In AD 1696-97 (AH 1108) orders were issued for the destruction of the major temples at Sorath in Gujarat. (…) He stopped public worship at the Hindu temple of Dwaraka'.

Herbert Esq., *Some Yeares Travels Into Africa & Asia The Great. Especially Describing the Famous Empires of Persia and Industant. As also Divers other Kingdoms in the Orientall Indies, And I'tes Adjacen*t.

(London:
Printed by R Bip. for Iacob Blome,
And Richard Bishop, 1638).
Sir Thomas Herbert, First Baronet, who visited Goa in
the seventeenth century writes,
'(...) as also the ruins of 2000 Idol Temples which the
Vice-Roy Antonio Norogna totally demolish, that no
memory might remain, or monuments continue, of such
gross Idolatry. For not only there, but at Salsette also were
two Temples or places of prophane Worship; one of them
(by incredible toil cut out of the hard Rock) was divided
into three Iles or Galleries, in which were figured many
of their deformed Pagotha's, and of which an Indian (if
to be credited) reports that there were in that Temple 300
of those narrow Galleries, and the Idols so exceeding ugly
as would affright an European Spectator; nevertheless
this was a celebrated place, and so abundantly frequented
by Idolators, as induced the Portuguise in zeal with a
considerable force to master the Town and to demolish
the Temples, breaking in pieces all that monstrous brood
of misshapen Pagods. In Goa nothing is more observable
now than the fortifications, the Vice-Roy and Arch-
bishops Palaces, and the Churches'.

13. Dr B.R. Ambedkar, *Pakistan or the Partition of India*
    (Bombay: Thacker and Co. Publishers, Third Edition,
    1946 (1940) Govt. of Maharashtra Reprint, 1990).
14. CIA, 'The World Factbook: Japan', https://www.cia.gov/
    the-world-factbook/countries/japan/.
15. Taittiriya Upanishad–Bhruguvalli-Anuvak 1.
16. https://globalpress.hinduismnow.org/magazine/agastyas-
    perfect-woman-lopamudra/.
17. Rajiv Malhotra and Satyanarayana Dasa Babaji, *Sanskrit
    Non-Translatables: The Importance of Sanskritizing
    English* (Delhi: Amaryllis, 2020).

18. *Bhagavad Gita: Commentary by Swami Mukundananda*, 'The Song of God', https://www.holy-bhagavad-gita.org/chapter/2/verse/47.
19. *Bhagavad Gita: Commentary by Swami Mukundananda*, 'The Song of God', https://www.holy-bhagavad-gita.org/chapter/2/verse/54.
20. *sthita-prajñasya kā bhāṣhā samādhi-sthasya keśhava sthita-dhīḥ kiṁ prabhāṣheta kim āsīta vrajeta kim vāsānsi jīrṇāni yathā vihāya navāni gṛihṇāti naro 'parāṇi tathā śharīrāṇi vihāya jīrṇānya nyāni sanyāti navāni dehī* https://www.holy-bhagavad-gita.org/chapter/2/verse/22
21. https://www.holy-bhagavad-gita.org/chapter/2/verse/47
22. Ibid.
23. Paraphrased from: Samyutta Nikaya–7.2 Akkosa Sutta
24. Swami Satyananda Saraswati, *Asana Pranayama Mudra Bandha* (Bihar: Yoga Publications Trust).
25. https://www.newsgram.com/general/2020/07/11/the-marriage-of-shiva-and-parvati-an-iconic-tale.
Sanskrit scholar Dr Mrunalini Nevalkar says:
'There is no Puranic reference to back this story. However, popular belief and temple rituals accept it to be so.
Kalikapurana says Lord Shiva and Goddess Parvati marry on the 5th day of bright half of Vaishakha – Shukla Paksha Panchami in the spring month of Vaisakha.'
26. Daniel J. Simmons and Christopher F. Chabris, 'Gorillas in our midst: sustained inattentional blindness for dynamic events', Department of Psychology, Harvard University, 20 June 1999, http://www.chabris.com/Simons1999.pdf.
27. https://lecerveau.mcgill.ca/flash/capsules/articles_pdf/triunebrain.pdf.

28. It's a key theological reason why other Gods, and particularly Goddesses, are not supposed to be worshipped in the non-pagan religions. The One Male God sees the Goddess as the source of sins, which is why even Eve is seen so negatively in the Adam and Eve story. This is not so in pagan religions, since most Gods are not jealous (and those that are, like Indra, are usually objects of ridicule). Also, the Goddesses are seen as very powerful. Also, God in the Abrahamic faith has called himself jealous. ('Thou shalt not bow down thyself to them, nor serve them: for I the LORD thy God am a jealous God, visiting the iniquity of the fathers upon the children unto the third and fourth generation of them that hate me.' Exodus 20:5)

29. Florence Minz and Dr Shruti Mishra, 'Ekam Sad Vipra Bahuda Vadanti: A Vedic Consciousness of God', December 2020, https://www.sieallahabad.org/hrt-admin/book/book_file/fd756770f9122be1b484f12c5ffbe828.pdf.

30. Tr. Swami Madhavananda, *Brihadaranyaka Upanishad with Commentary of Shankaracarya* (Almora: Advaita Ashrama, 3rd Edition, 1950).

31. Ed. Dr Ganganath Jha, *Chandogya Upanishad with Shankara Bhashya* (Pune: Oriental Book Agency, 1st Edition, 1942).

32. Joseph Campbell, *The Power of Myth*.

33. Ibid. (pp. 110–112).

34. https://en.wikipedia.org/wiki/The_Lion_King.

35. Tr. Pritish Nandy, *Isha Upanishad* (Kolkata: Seagull Books, 2018).

36. https://hazen.carnegiescience.edu/research/evolutionary-system-mineralogy.

37. https://philarchive.org/archive/LITCO-11.

38. M.A. Gartstein and M.K. Skinner, 'Prenatal influences on temperament development: The role of environmental epigenetics', *Development and Psychopathology*, 30(4), 2018, 1269–1303. https://doi.org/10.1017/S095457941700173040.

39. Siddhartha Mukherjee, *The Gene: An Intimate History* (US: Allen Lane, Penguin Group, 2016).

40. Stephen Weaver, *Greek Gods: The Olympians* (California: CreateSpace Independent Publishing Platform, September 2015).
    https://www.greek-gods.info/greek-gods/zeus/stories/zeus-king-of-the-gods/.

41. Dietrich Boschung, *Kairos As A Figuration of Time: A Case Study*, 2013, https://brill.com/display/title/51481.

42. https://d-nb.info/1142372448/34.

43. Manoj Chalam, https://www.youtube.com/watch?v=VHaqcuL5-kA&t=224s.

44. Dan Brown, *The Da Vinci Code* (London: Transworld Publishers).

45. https://en.wikipedia.org/wiki/Gone_with_the_Wind_(film).
    https://en.wikipedia.org/wiki/Chariots_of_Fire.
    https://en.wikipedia.org/wiki/Guide_(film).

46. https://en.wikipedia.org/wiki/The_Bourne_Identity_(1988_film).

47. Sandhya Jain and Meenakshi Jain, *The India They Saw Complete Series* (Delhi: Prabhat Prakashan, 2022).

48. Stephan Weaver, *Greek Gods: The Olympians* (California: CreateSpace Independent Publishing Platform, September 2015).

49. https://www.greeka.com/greece-myths/king-midas/.

50. https://www.britannica.com/topic/Pandora-Greek-mythology.
https://www.theoi.com/Ther/AetosKaukasios.html.
https://www.theoi.com/Titan/TitanPrometheus.html.

51. Joseph Campbell, 'Myth as the Mirror for the Ego', *YouTube*, 27 August 2010, https://www.youtube.com/watch?v=VgOUxICCHoA.

52. Shiva Purana—Rudra Samhita, Kumara Khanda, Adhyaya 13, i.e., Shiva Purana II.4.13.

53. Manoj Chalam, https://www.youtube.com/watch?v=7fRKY rO6J7Q&t=1224s.

54. Yajnavalkya Smriti Acharadhyaya, Ganapati Kalpa Prakarana, i.e. Yajnavalkya Smriti I. 11.

55. https://www.ibpbooks.com/iconography-of-vinayaka-ganapati-and-ganesa/p/15405.
Haripriya Rangarajan, *Iconography of Vinayaka, Ganapati and Ganesa* (2014).
Yajnavalkya Smriti Acharadhyaya, Ganapati Kalpa Prakarana, i.e. Yajnavalkya Smriti I. 11.

56. Manoj Chalam, https://www.youtube.com/watch?v=VHaqcuL5-kA&list=RDCMUCNkkYUlu1_A5y0M2u bN8aPw&start_radio=1&rv=VHaqcuL5-kA&t=1095.

57. https://www.shreemaa.org/story-narada-curses-vishnu/
https://www.researchut.com/hindu-mythology/narada-curse-lord-vishnu-2/#gsc.tab=0.

58. https://vedicfeed.com/curses-of-durvasa-rishi/.
Devdutt Pattaniak, *Shyam: An Illustrated retelling of the Bhagavata* (Delhi: Penguin, 2018).

59. Yoga also translates these as ripples of the mind. Often it explains Chitta as a serene lake. Vrittis are the ripples in the otherwise calm lake of mind.
Yoga Sutra I.2 योगश्चित्तवृत्तिनिरोधः । explains Yoga as a method that helps one exercise control on these ripples of mind.

Manoj Chalam, https://www.youtube.com/watch?v=7fRKYrO6J7Q&t=1224s.

https://www.youtube.com/watch?v=VHaqcuL5-kA&list=RDCMUCNkkYUlu1_A5y0M2ubN8aPw&start_radio=1&rv=VHaqcuL5-kA&t=1095.

60. https://www.ibpbooks.com/iconography-of-vinayaka-ganapati-and-ganesa/p/15405.

Haripriya Rangarajan, *Iconography of Vinayaka, Ganapati and Ganesa* (2014).

Yajnavalkya Smriti Acharadhyaya, Ganapati Kalpa Prakarana, i.e. Yajnavalkya Smriti I. 11.

61. Markandeyapurana Chap.82

62. Manoj Chalam, https://www.youtube.com/watch?v=VHaqcuL5-kA&t=224s.

63. https://www.britannica.com/topic/Hydra-Greek-mythology.

https://chandra.si.edu/photo/constellations/hydra.html#:~:text=The%20Hydra%20was%20a%20fresh, Tiamat%20and%20the%20Hebrew%20Rahab.

64. Shri Satyanarayan Vrat Katha and Aarti—श्री सत्यनारायण व्रत कथा एवं आरती (ishwarpooja.com).

श्री सत्यनारायण व्रत कथा (Shrisatyanarayan Vrat Katha) (gitapressbookshop.in).

Sadhguru and Arundhati Subramanium, *Adiyogi: The Source of Yoga* (Delhi: HarperCollins India, 2017).

65. Adi Shankaracharya, *The Works of Sri Sankaracharya*, Vol.16, Nirvana Shatakam/ Atma Shatakam (Srirangam: Sri Vani Vilas Editions, 1910) pp. 61-65.

66. Aashish A. Bardekar, 'Analysis of Indian Classical Raga Yaman on Human Brain Waves', *IJCRT*, Volume 6 Issue 3, April 2018, https://ijcrt.org/papers/IJCRT1893254.pdf.

67. https://dbpedia.org/page/Shree_(Hindustani_raga)
    https://meetkalakar.com/Artipedia/raga-marwa

68. Shambhavi L. Chopra, *Yogic Secrets of the Dark Goddess* (Wisdom Tree, 2007).

69. Goddess Durga celebrated during the Navaratri as symbolizing mastery over the emotions of anger, pain, fear, among others, as the navarasa: https://timesofindia. indiatimes.com/blogs/tea-with-life/navratri-is-the-festival-to-control-nine-emotions/
    Manoj Chalam calls Goddess Durga "Goodness in a fierce form": https://www.youtube.com/watch?v=VHaqcuL5-kA
    48:52 https://www.youtube.com/watch?v=nC6jJh-1sYA Ma Durga helps face and conquer emotions like krodh (anger), darr/ bhaya (fear), moh (attachments), lobha (greed) and others:
    https://lifecoachprafulla.blogspot.com/2019/10/maa-durga-navratri-celebration.html

70. Shambhavi L. Chopra, *Yogic Secrets of the Dark Goddess* (Wisdom Tree, 2007).

71. Ibid.

72. Ibid.

73. Sadhguru and Arundhati Subramanium, *Adiyogi: The Source of Yoga* (Delhi: HarperCollins India, 2017).

74. https://www.timelessmyths.com/gods/chinese/erlang-shen/.
    http://www.bjreview.com/Lifestyle/201802/t20180209_800117196.html.

75. Skanda Purana II. 4.35 Vaishnava Khanda, Kartika Masa Mahatmya, Chap. 35.

76. https://kalyanikalamandir.com/blogs/forms-of-tandava/
    https://icctmemphis.org/information/temple-campus/sapta-tandavas/.

77. https://ghungrookathakacademy.com/wp-content/uploads/2021/07/Tandav-and-Lasya.pdf.
https://en.wikipedia.org/wiki/Tandava.

78. Skanda Purana II. 4.35 Vaishnava Khanda, Kartika Masa Mahatmya, Chap. 35.
The same chapter talks about death of Tripura at the hands of Lord Shiva. But it does not talks about Tripura Tandava.

79. Manoj Chalam, 'The Power of Hindu & Buddhist Deities in Yoga',
https://www.youtube.com/watch?v=VHaqcuL5-kA&list=RDCMUCNkkYUlu1_A5y0M2ubN8aPw&start_radio=1&rv=VHaqcuL5-kA&t=1095.

80. https://swarajyamag.com/ideas/the-nataraja-and-epilepsy-an-interpretation-of-the-cosmic-dancer.

81. Anand Venkatraman, 'The Nataraja and Epilepsy: An Interpretation of the Cosmic Dancer', *Swarajya*, 19 May 2018, https://swarajyamag.com/ideas/the-nataraja-and-epilepsy-an-interpretation-of-the-cosmic-dancer.

82. https://lecerveau.mcgill.ca/flash/capsules/articles_pdf/triunebrain.pdf.

83. https://www.britannica.com/topic/Tlazolteotl
https://spiralworlds.com/index/gods/mesoamerican-pantheon/tlazolteotl/

84. Thomas A. Harris, MD, *I'm OK – You're OK* (London: Random House).

85. Manoj Chalam, https://www.youtube.com/watch?v=VHaqcuL5-kA&list=RDCMUCNkkYUlu1_A5y0M2ubN8aPw&start_radio=1&rv=VHaqcuL5-kA&t=1095.

86. Ibid.

87. Kurma Purana Purva Bhaga Adhyaya 1 verses 27–40, i.e., Kurma Purana 1.1.27–40
Padma Purana II.1.4

88. Manoj Chalam, https://www.youtube.com/watch?v=VHaqcuL5-kA&list=RDCMUCNkkYUlu1_A5y0M2ubN8aPw&start_radio=1&rv=VHaqcuL5-kA&t=1095.

89. https://resanskrit.com/blogs/blog-post/celebrating-raksha-bandhan.

90. Vamanapurana, Ch. 65, 49, Saromahatmya Chap. 2–10.

91. Shiva as an Archer found in Aitareya Brahmana 13.9.33.

92. *Mrugha vyadha,* the hunter of deer, is an epithet of Lord Shiva, and also one of the 11 Rudras.

93. Purana Sati Khanda 2.13 i.e., Shiva V.2.13.
    Skanda Purana Vaishnava Khanda, Badarikashrama Mahatmya, Ch. 2, I.e., Skanda II.3.2.
    Bhavishya Purana III.4.13.

94. Manoj Chalam, https://www.youtube.com/watch?v=VHaqcuL5-kA&list=RDCMUCNkkYUlu1_A5y0M2ubN8aPw&start_radio=1&rv=VHaqcuL5-kA&t=1095.

95. Manoj Chalam, 'Duet of One', https://www.youtube.com/watch?v=VHaqcuL5-kA&t=224s.

96. Devdutt Pattanaik, *Shyam, An Illustrated Retelling of the Bhagavata* (Delhi: Penguin Random House India, 2018).

97. Marathi poetess Sneha Datar.

98. https://mythologyandvaishbhat.wordpress.com/2021/08/30/parijata-the-flower-from-heaven/.

99. Pritish Nandy, *Isha Upanishad* (Seagull Books, 2018).

100. http://www.actualization.in/2020/12/love-indic-perspective.html.

101. Bhagavata Purana Skandha 10, Chapters 80–81

102. Marathi poetess Sneha Datar.

103. Ed. T. Ganpati Sastri, *Dramas of Bhasa, Trivandrum Sanskrit Series No. XXII* (1912).

104. Valmiki Ramayana III.49 ff.

105. https://www.greeklegendsandmyths.com/echo-and-narcissus.html.

106. Coleman Barks, *Rumi: The Book of Love*, *Diwan-e Shams-e Tabrizi*.

107. https://www.amazon.in/India-Sacred-Geography-Diana-Eck/dp/0385531907.

108. The following PhD thesis, along with a bibliography at the end of the thesis
"Thesis (P-755).pdf"

109. It is an auspicious Rangoli like a magic square 3x3 where numbers tally to 72.

110. This is also a magic square 4x4 which accounts to 34.

111. The minorities in Pakistan have died of genocide over the last seventy-five years (from approximately 23 per cent to 3–4 per cent of the population today, according to Pakistani scholar Farahnaz Ispahani). This is a far bigger genocide than what the Jews suffered under the Nazis. Pakistan also carried out a massive genocide in Bangladesh in 1971. In India, Nepal, etc., minority proportions of population have gone up over the same period. Similarly true for most countries in the West, also UAE, Indonesia, etc., where minority proportions of the populations have also gone up. Many countries, including even some in the much derided Middle East, are not as bad as they are made out to be. On the other hand, Pakistan is really among the worst countries in human history for minorities.
Farahnaz Ispahani, *Purifying the Land of the Pure: Pakistan's Religious Minorities* (Delhi: HarperCollins India, 1 December 2016).

Other Titles by Amish

The Shiva Trilogy

The fastest-selling book series in the history of Indian publishing

THE IMMORTALS OF MELUHA
(Book 1 of the Trilogy)

1900 BC. What modern Indians mistakenly call the Indus Valley Civilisation, the inhabitants of that period knew as the land of Meluha – a near perfect empire created many centuries earlier by Lord Ram. Now their primary river Saraswati is drying, and they face terrorist attacks from their enemies from the east. Will their prophesied hero, the Neelkanth, emerge to destroy evil?

THE SECRET OF THE NAGAS
(Book 2 of the Trilogy)

The sinister Naga warrior has killed his friend Brahaspati and now stalks his wife Sati. Shiva, who is the prophesied destroyer of evil, will not rest till he finds his demonic adversary. His thirst for revenge will lead him to the door of the Nagas, the serpent people. Fierce battles will be fought and unbelievable secrets revealed in the second part of the Shiva trilogy.

THE OATH OF THE VAYUPUTRAS
(Book 3 of the Trilogy)

Shiva reaches the Naga capital, Panchavati, and prepares for a holy war against his true enemy. The Neelkanth must not fail, no matter what the cost. In his desperation, he reaches out to the Vayuputras. Will he succeed? And what will be the real cost of battling Evil? Read the concluding part of this bestselling series to find out.

The Ram Chandra Series

RAM – SCION OF IKSHVAKU
(Book 1 of the Series)

He loves his country and he stands alone for the law. His band of brothers, his wife, Sita and the fight against the darkness of chaos. He is Prince Ram. Will he rise above the taint that others heap on him? Will his love for Sita sustain him through his struggle? Will he defeat the demon Raavan who destroyed his childhood? Will he fulfil the destiny of the Vishnu? Begin an epic journey with Amish's latest: the Ram Chandra Series.

SITA – WARRIOR OF MITHILA
(Book 2 of the Series)

An abandoned baby is found in a field. She is adopted by the ruler of Mithila, a powerless kingdom, ignored by all. Nobody believes this child will amount to much. But they are wrong. For she is no ordinary girl. She is Sita. Through an innovative multi-linear narrative, Amish takes you deeper into the epic world of the Ram Chandra Series.

RAAVAN – ENEMY OF ARYAVARTA
(Book 3 of the Series)

Raavan is determined to be a giant among men, to conquer, plunder, and seize the greatness that he thinks is his right. He is a man of contrasts, of brutal violence and scholarly knowledge. A man who will love without reward and kill without remorse. In this, the third book in the Ram Chandra series, Amish sheds light on Raavan, the king of Lanka. Is he the greatest villain in history or just a man in a dark place, all the time?

WAR OF LANKA
(Book 4 of the Series)

As Raavan kidnaps Sita, Ram seethes with rage and grief. The war of Lanka is imminent; it's a war for Dharma, after all. Will Ram defeat the ruthless and seemingly invincible Raavan? Or will Lanka fight back like a cornered tiger? And, most importantly, will the real Vishnu rise? In this fourth book of the Ram Chandra Series, the narrative strands of Ram, Sita, and Ravana crash into each other and explode in a slaughterous war.

Indic Chronicles

LEGEND OF SUHELDEV

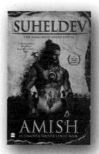

Repeated attacks by Mahmud of Ghazni have weakened India's northern regions. Then the Turks raid and destroy one of the holiest temples in the land: the magnificent Lord Shiva temple at Somnath. At this most desperate of times, a warrior rises to defend the nation. King Suheldev—fierce rebel, charismatic leader, inclusive patriot. Read this epic adventure of courage and heroism that recounts the story of that lionhearted warrior and the magnificent Battle of Bahraich.

Non-fiction

IMMORTAL INDIA

Explore India with the country's storyteller, Amish, who helps you understand it like never before, through a series of sharp articles, nuanced speeches and intelligent debates. In *Immortal India*, Amish lays out the vast landscape of an ancient culture with a fascinatingly modern outlook.

DHARMA – DECODING THE EPICS FOR A MEANINGFUL LIFE

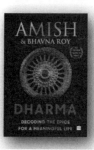

In this genre-bending book, the first of a series, Amish and Bhavna dive into the priceless treasure trove of the ancient Indian epics, as well as the vast and complex universe of Amish's Meluha, to explore some of the key concepts of Indian philosophy. Within this book are answers to our many philosophical questions, offered through simple and wise interpretations of our favourite stories.

30 Years *of*

 HarperCollins *Publishers* India

At HarperCollins, we believe in telling the best stories and finding the widest possible readership for our books in every format possible. We started publishing 30 years ago; a great deal has changed since then, but what has remained constant is the passion with which our authors write their books, the love with which readers receive them, and the sheer joy and excitement that we as publishers feel in being a part of the publishing process.

Over the years, we've had the pleasure of publishing some of the finest writing from the subcontinent and around the world, and some of the biggest bestsellers in India's publishing history. Our books and authors have won a phenomenal range of awards, and we ourselves have been named Publisher of the Year the greatest number of times. But nothing has meant more to us than the fact that millions of people have read the books we published, and somewhere, a book of ours might have made a difference.

As we step into our fourth decade, we go back to that one word – a word which has been a driving force for us all these years.

Read.

Harper
Collins

HARPER
PERENNIAL

HARPER
BUSINESS

HARPER
BLACK

हार्पर
हिन्दी

HarperCollins
Children's Books

HARPER
DESIGN

HARPER
VANTAGE

Harper
Sport